50 AMAZING THINGS KIDS NEED TO KNOW ABOUT SCIENCE

50 AMAZING THINGS THINGS KIDS NEED TO KNOW ABOUT SCIENCE

PENNY JOHNSON

Sky Pony Press
New York

CONTENTS

INTRODUCTION

Have you ever wished that you could make yourself invisible? Would you like to be a little smarter or even a bit stronger? Perhaps you would rather spend your time looking for other planets. But if you found one, would you be able to live there?

These questions may seem strange to you and you may think they are even a little ridiculous, but scientists think about these types of bizarre question all the time!

This book explains how many of these and other questions have already been answered by scientists. By understanding the facts behind their research and by working and gathering information, you will start to think like a scientist and will probably come up with some strange questions of your own. Who knows, you may even discover something useful along the way!

Before you can start your journey towards making your ground-breaking discovery, you need to know a bit more about the science behind some of the issues facing people today. For example, there's no point trying to save the planet without figuring out how you are going feed everyone on it.

It is packed with useful hints and tips. You can even see how things work in practice by doing the "see for yourself" experiments. For example, you can find the best material to stop something warming up or see how to make a bottle of fizzy drink explode! You can read the whole book or just the chapters that you find interesting, but once you start, you will probably want to keep reading!

This may involve finding out how to make it rain in drought-stricken areas or how to generate non-polluting electricity from sunshine. Similarly, if you know how to survive in the Arctic or on a desert island, climb the highest mountains, or dive to the bottom of the ocean, you are just about prepared for anything and everything that the scientific world can throw at you!

This book will put all the facts at your fingertips. Each chapter looks at a different scientific idea, from those based on physics and chemistry to biology and geography. It will study how these scientific ideas affect the real world and how you can use science to change the world around you.

Science allows us to explain the world around us. It can help us to build cars and computers and help us to develop medicines to cure us when we are ill. It can also help people to get to the bottom of the ocean or out into the depths of space. Using science to find out things can be inspiring, exciting, and, most importantly, a lot of fun.

HOW TO BE AN ANIMAL TRACKER

Badger

Cat

Lots of animals live around us, even in towns and cities. You cannot always see the animals because many avoid humans or come out only at night. But you can often find out which animals have been around by looking for the tracks they leave in mud or snow.

Giraffe

Sheep

RECORDING TRACKS

The drawings on this page show the shapes of the footprints left by different animals and birds. Some of the prints are easy to identify, such as the tracks left by horses. But you might find some prints that you cannot identify right away.

The best way to find out about these is to record the tracks so that you can look them up later.

TAKE A PICTURE

If you have a camera, take a photo of the tracks. Put a ruler on the ground next to them, so you can use the photograph to work out how big they are. This will help you to

Dog

Duck

Fox

Hedgehog

identify them later. If you do not have a ruler, put something like a pencil or even a coin next to them for scale. You can also make a sketch of the tracks in a notebook. Remember to record the size if you do this.

Horse

DROPPINGS

You can also find out about the animals that have been in an area by looking for their droppings. Rabbits and sheep leave round droppings about 0.4 inch (1 cm) in across. Fox droppings (called scats) look like dog droppings, but are whiter as they contain animal bones. Some animals that do not normally leave footprints, such as owls, leave pellets containing fur and bones from the small mammals they have eaten.

Crow

Rabbit

Human

Squirrel

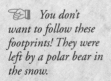
☞ *You don't want to follow these footprints! They were left by a polar bear in the snow.*

see for yourself

The pattern of the tracks left by an animal can sometimes tell you if it is running or walking, or how big the animal is. Find an area of muddy ground or damp sand, and walk along it. Measure the distance between your footprints. Now make another set of footprints by running and see how much further apart your steps are.

Wolf

2 HOW TO LOOK AT THE BACK OF YOUR HEAD

You can see your own face by looking into a mirror, but this is not quite how other people see you. You can even use mirrors to see around walls, but can you use them to see the back of your head?

HOW MIRRORS WORK

Some things—such as light bulbs, the Sun, or even a television screen—make their own light, but most things do not. Instead you see them when light is reflected by them (bounces off them) and goes into your eyes.

Mirrors are very good at reflecting light. They reflect light evenly, so when you see light that has been reflected by a mirror, you see an image of the things in front of the mirror. When you look into a mirror, light from the Sun or a light bulb bounces off your face towards the mirror. The mirror reflects the light back towards your eyes, so you see an image of your face. If you want to see the back of your head, you need to use two mirrors.

LEFT AND RIGHT IN MIRRORS

When you look at something in a mirror, left and right appear to be swapped around. You can easily see this by holding up this book to a mirror—the writing you see in the mirror will be backwards.

This chimp recognizes that the image in the mirror is himself. Most animals think the image is another animal.

This means that the image of yourself that you see in the mirror is not the same as the way other people see you. You can look at yourself as others see you by holding two mirrors at right angles to each other.

UP PERISCOPE!

You can see around corners or over walls using mirrors. To look around a corner, hold a mirror just beyond the corner and tilt it so that you can see what is happening. You need a periscope to look over a wall. Make a periscope using two mirrors, a cardboard tube, and some tape. You will also need a pair of scissors.

Cut two slits in the tube at 45 degrees and fasten the mirrors in these slits using tape

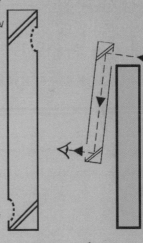

Cut holes in the sides of the tube opposite the mirrors—you may need to adjust the angles of the two mirrors

You can use your periscope to look over walls or other opaque objects.

3 HOW TO GO REALLY FAST

The fastest people on the planet can run at more than 33 ft (10 m) per second and cycle at more than 80 mph (130 km/h). To go faster than this you need an engine. And for really fast speeds you would need to strap yourself to a powerful rocket—and cross your fingers!

AIR RESISTANCE

There are forces on almost all moving things that try to slow these things down. If something is sliding along the ground, there is friction between that object and the ground. And there are forces that slow down things even when they are not touching the ground. This is because of air resistance. The only moving things that are not affected by air resistance are rockets and satellites out in space, where there is no air!

If you stand outside on a windy day, you can feel the force of the wind pushing you. You get the same effect if you move through the air quickly. When you are going fast on a bicycle you can feel the air pushing on you, trying to slow you down. The faster you go, the bigger the air resistance.

WATER RESISTANCE

You get the same effect in water. However, because water is denser than

The X-15 holds the record for the fastest airplane. Powered by a rocket engine, this plane could roar to 4,350 mph (7,000 km/h).

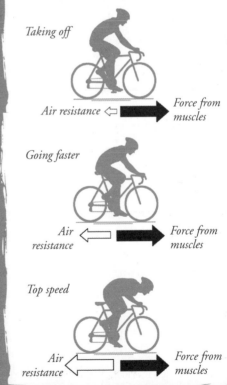

You need a force to get things moving. When you cycle, the force is provided by your leg muscles. They make you accelerate (go faster). The faster you go, the greater the air resistance. The force from your muscles has to balance out the air resistance. Eventually you go so fast that the resistance is the same as the force from your muscles, and you cannot go any faster. This is your top speed.

Taking off

Air resistance ⇐   *Force from muscles*

Going faster

Air resistance ⇐   *Force from muscles*

Top speed

Air resistance ⇐   *Force from muscles*

air (there is more of it in a certain space) water resistance is much greater than air resistance. This is one reason why the speed record for boats is only 318 mph (511 km/h).

Special helmet gives a more streamlined shape

Tight clothes and covers over the wheel spokes allow the air to flow past smoothly

Crouching over the handlebars makes a smaller area for the air to hit

If you want to go faster, you need to make your air resistance as small as possible. You can do this by making your area smaller, by wearing smooth clothes instead of flappy jackets and baggy shorts, and by having a smooth, "streamlined" shape to make it easy for the air to flow past you.

Cyclists try to make themselves streamlined to move through the air as easily as possible. They usually wear streamlined helmets and hunch over their handlebars. This means they need to use less muscle power to move around.

WIND TUNNELS

Designers of cars or airplanes need to find out how much air resistance their design will have. This is very difficult to measure while something is moving, so instead they use a wind tunnel where the car or airplane stays still and air is blown past it. Airplanes are too big to fit into wind tunnels, so engineers test models instead.

Engineers can use streams of smoke in the wind tunnel to help them see how the air moves past the car. They can also put the car on a special mounting that measures the forces on the car caused by the moving air. Even cyclists and other athletes use wind tunnels—for example, to test their clothing or to find the best body position for getting their air resistance as low as possible.

USING GRAVITY

Gravity pulls things towards the center of the Earth. This means that if you are on a bicycle on a hill, gravity will pull you down the hill without any effort from you. If you pedal as well, you can go really fast.

Skiers use gravity to accelerate down snowy slopes. The fastest speed for a downhill skier is over 155 mph (250 km/h). Skiers put special wax on their skis to reduce the friction between the skis and the snow. They also crouch down to reduce their area, and wear special helmets and clothes to give them a streamlined shape.

GOING FASTER

Every car has a top speed that depends on the amount of air resistance it produces when it is moving, and how much force its engine can produce. If the car is made more streamlined it can go faster before the air resistance force becomes big enough to balance the force from its engine. A car can also be made to go faster by giving it a more powerful engine. This produces a much bigger force.

In 1997, a car called *ThrustSSC* was the first car to go faster than the speed of sound. To go this fast it had to have a very streamlined shape with a small front area, and very powerful engines. Normal car engines were not powerful enough so *ThrustSSC* used two jet engines from a fighter airplane!

Fast cars need to have a streamlined body so that they cut through the air as easily as possible.

4 HOW TO CROSS AN OCEAN

Over half of the Earth is covered in water. People have been using boats on rivers and lakes for thousands of years, but how do you build a boat that can get across thousands of miles of open ocean?

ROWING POWER

In 1896, Frank Samuelsen and George Harbo became the first people to row across the Atlantic Ocean. It took them an arm-aching 55 days. Since then many other people have rowed across the Atlantic, and today there is even a race held every two years. The first people to row across the even bigger Pacific Ocean arrived in Australia in 1972. Their exhausting voyage had taken nearly a year!

SOMETHING BIGGER

But rowing is not a very practical way to cross an ocean. The rowing boats used in the Atlantic rowing race are big enough only to carry the rowers and their food.

Do you think these two sailors will get all the way across an ocean in this boat?

They cannot carry passengers or cargo. Something a little larger is needed for that—requiring something a little more powerful than oars to push it along.

FLOATING AND SINKING

You can predict whether a material will float or sink if you know its density. If you take pieces of wood and metal that are the same size, you can feel that the metal is heavier. The metal has a higher density, which means that it has more mass than the wood for the same volume. If a material is more dense than water it will sink. If it is less dense than water it will float.

Most metals are more dense than water, so you might think that a ship made out of steel will sink. Not so! If you are thinking about ships, you need to take into account all the air spaces inside the ship as well. The overall density of a ship is less than the density of water.

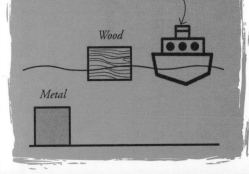

Overall density of the ship is less than the density of water

Wood

Metal

Sailing into the wind

Clippers are "square-rigged" ships. These can sail only if the wind is behind them. Modern yachts are "fore-and-aft-rigged," with one edge of the sail fixed to the mast or to the forestay (a wire running from the mast to the front of the boat). Fore-and-aft-rigged boats can sail towards the wind.

The wind is forced to change direction as it flows over the sail, and this produces a force on the sail. This force tries to push the boat sideways. The boat also has a large keel that sticks down into the water. As the boat tries to move sideways the keel is pulled through the water, and this makes a force in the opposite direction. The combination of the two forces makes the boat go forwards. No sailing boats can sail directly into the wind, but modern yachts can sail about 45 degrees from the wind direction.

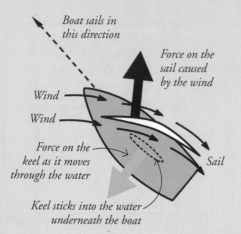

Boat sails in this direction

Force on the sail caused by the wind

Wind

Wind

Force on the keel as it moves through the water

Sail

Keel sticks into the water underneath the boat

Viking longship

VIKING VOYAGERS

The first people to cross the Atlantic were probably the Vikings, more than 1,000 years ago. Viking longships had sails and oars. They used the sails whenever the wind was blowing in the right direction. Later ships were bigger, with more sails. Wind blowing on the sails provides a force to push a ship along. The more sails there are, the faster the ship goes, as long as the masts and the rigging (the ropes that hold up the sails and masts) are strong enough to withstand the winds!

SHIPS WITH ENGINES

The first ship with an engine to cross the Atlantic Ocean was the SS *Savannah*, in 1819. The SS *Savannah* had sails as well

18

Clipper

Yacht

as a steam engine. The first ship that was built to take passengers across the Atlantic using steam power alone was the SS *Great Western*, which made her first crossing in 1838. All these ships had to carry a large amount of coal as well as their passengers and cargo. The coal was burned in furnaces, and the heat from the burning coal was used to boil water and turn it into steam. The steam made the engine turn.

PADDLE OR PROPELLER

The early steamships used their engines to turn huge paddle wheels on the outside of the ship. Later ships had much smaller propellers, under the water near the back of the ship.

GOING NUCLEAR

Even some modern ships use steam power, but they use nuclear power to heat water to make steam. Most modern ships use diesel-powered engines—a bit like the engines in trucks and buses, but much, much bigger!

see for yourself

Make a boat out of modelling clay. Boats are only useful if they can carry people and cargo, so see how many coins or other small objects your boat can carry without sinking. Use the same amount of clay, but try out some different shapes to see which shape can hold the most coins.

HOW TO READ SOMEONE'S MIND

Knowing exactly what someone is thinking is called "telepathy." As far as we know, telepathy does not exist. Although you cannot read someone's mind, you **can** have an idea about what other people are thinking.

INVESTIGATING TELEPATHY

Many people claim to be able to read other people's minds. However, scientists have carried out many tests on such people and so far no one has really been able to do this. One way of testing a "telepath" is to show a person one of a set of cards, like the ones below.

By using these cards, you can test whether a person can actually read another person's mind or is just having a very lucky guess.

He or she then tries to "send" the image of the card to a person sitting in another room.

This second person has to say which card the first person is looking at. If the second person just guessed, he or she might expect to make the right choice in one out of every five guesses. When this test has been carried out, no one has managed to guess any better than this.

READING FEELINGS FROM FACES

You might not know exactly what someone is thinking, but you can often tell what they are feeling. For example, if someone is crying, you can probably tell that he or she is unhappy. People have different expressions on their faces when they have different feelings. You can usually tell if someone is feeling angry, surprised, or frightened.

There is also a "body language" that can show what someone is feeling. Some body language messages are so clear that you can even tell these stick men are "feeling," even though you know they are just drawings!

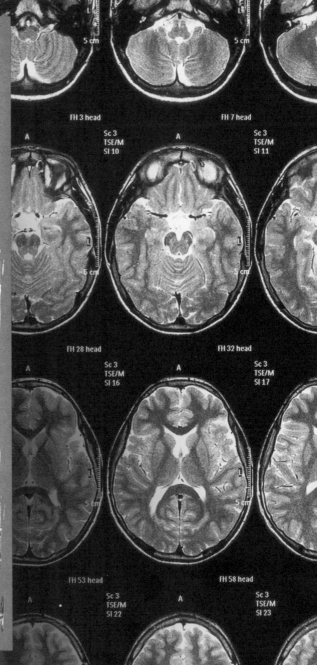

CLEVER HANS

Wilhelm von Osten used to show people how clever his horse, Hans, was by asking him to do sums. Hans would tap his hoof the right number of times to give the answer. It turned out that Hans could not do arithmetic, but was good at reading the body language of the person asking the question. For example, if the answer was eight, the person asking the question would change the expression on his face or move his body a little as the horse tapped for the eighth time. This happened because the person asking the questions was hoping Hans would stop there and get the right answer. Hans could see this change, so he knew to stop tapping. Von Osten was not a cheat—he really believed his horse was clever. He did not even know he was changing his body language. Hans could do his tricks for anyone, as long as the person asking the question knew the answer. The horse was better at reading body language than the people were!

LOCKED-IN PATIENTS

After a bad accident or after certain kinds of illness, some patients can be awake but not able to talk. They can sometimes move their eyes or swallow, but they cannot communicate with their families or nurses. Until very recently there was no way of finding out whether or not these patients knew what was happening around them.

In 2010, doctors were able to communicate with one of these patients for the first time. They put the patient in a brain scanner and asked him some questions. If the answer was "yes" he had to think about playing tennis. If the answer was "no" he had to think about walking around the rooms in his house.

Thinking about these things uses different areas of the brain. The brain scanner can detect which parts of the brain are being used more than others, so doctors could use the scans to work out if the patient was saying "yes" or "no." The patient answered simple questions correctly.

This method is not really mind reading—it can tell only which of two different things a person is thinking about. And it works only on some people. But it is better for the patients than not being able to communicate at all. One day it may be possible for people like this to control a computer by thinking about different things.

By using MRI (magnetic resonance imaging), doctors can see inside a patient's brain.

see for yourself

Pretend you can read someone's mind. Ask them to think of a number, but not to tell you what it is. Ask them to double their number and then add ten. Then they divide this answer by two and take away the number they first thought of. Make your trick more convincing by asking them to think hard about their final answer, before telling them that it is five. The answer will always be half the number you asked them to add.

6 HOW TO BE A FORENSIC SCIENTIST

There has been a robbery! How do the police find the criminals? Sometimes the police have to rely on tiny clues. Forensic scientists try to find out who committed a crime. They use lots of different evidence to solve crimes, including soil and bugs!

GATHERING EVIDENCE

When a crime is discovered, forensic scientists help the police to find evidence. This might be footprints, things a criminal has dropped, or soil or other substances that may have been on the criminal's shoes. Pollen and soil on the victim, or even tiny fibers from carpets or other fabrics, can also be important clues. The criminal may also have left fingerprints on objects at the crime scene. All the evidence must be carefully recorded, including where and when it was found. Once detectives think they have worked out who committed the crime, that person will be taken to court. The evidence gathered will then be used to show whether or not he or she is guilty.

SOIL SAMPLES

Murdered bodies are often buried. If the police have a suspect, they may search the person's car, home, clothes, and shoes

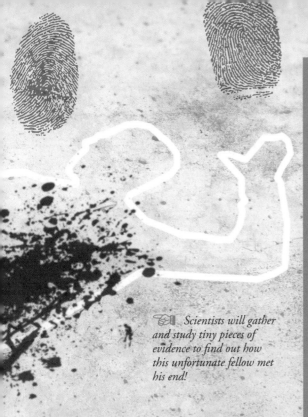

FINGERPRINTS

If you look at the tips of your fingers you can see swirling lines. These are your fingerprints. When you touch something, oils in your skin get left on the surface in the pattern of these lines. Forensic scientists can see these "prints" by dusting surfaces with powder, which sticks to the oil. The prints can then be lifted off using a sticky plastic, or can be photographed. Everyone's fingerprints are unique, so these patterns can be used to identify people.

If someone has broken into your house, the police will look for fingerprints. They will also take fingerprints from everyone at the house, to rule out any prints belonging to the householders.

Scientists will gather and study tiny pieces of evidence to find out how this unfortunate fellow met his end!

and sometimes they find some soil samples. Soils are different in different places, and forensic scientists can use chemical tests to identify different soils. If there is soil from the place where the body is buried on the suspect or on his or her car, that is evidence that the criminal could have been at the crime scene. It does not prove that he or she *was* the murderer, only that they had been in the same place.

see for yourself

You can collect your own fingerprints. Press your fingers against a window or mirror. Now you need to blow some powder onto the glass. A large make-up brush and face powder works well. Get some powder on the brush, and move it gently across the glass. You can also try blowing talcum powder or flour onto the glass.

COLLECTING POLLEN

Pollen can also provide evidence that a person has been to a particular place. Pollen is produced by plants as part of their life cycle, and each kind of plant has a different kind of pollen. Grass is everywhere, so grass pollen on a suspect's clothes is not very helpful. However, if the suspect has grains of pollen from the same plants that are growing in the victim's garden, then they were probably in that garden at some time.

WHEN DID THEY DIE?

Detectives need to find out when a murder victim died, so that they can work out who might have killed them. A forensic pathologist will examine a dead body carefully to find out how, and roughly when, the person died. For example, if

Using insects

If a body has been dead for more than a few days, insects can sometimes help in working out when the person died. For example, flies and beetles lay eggs in dead meat (including human corpses), and the eggs hatch into maggots. Forensic entomologists use clues from insects to help solve crimes, and they can tell from the size of the maggots how long ago the eggs were laid. The person must have been dead for at least this long.

food in the stomach has not been digested, the person must have died shortly after eating their last meal.

GOING COLD

The bodies of humans and other mammals are warm, because of all the chemical reactions that happen inside them to keep them alive. When a person dies, these reactions stop and the body gradually cools down. A forensic pathologist can take the temperature of a dead body to help work out how long ago the person died. Muscles in the body also become stiffer and stiffer for 12 hours after the person dies. This is called rigor mortis. It gradually wears off again over the next three days. So the pathologist can also estimate the time of death from how stiff the body is.

FIBERS

Detectives often find fibers from carpets or clothing at a crime scene. Fibers can be made of different materials, and the type of material can often be identified using a microscope. This can help forensic scientists to match up the fiber with materials found in a suspect's home or car.

PAINT

Tiny flecks of paint can also be important clues. For example, detectives might suspect that some bits of red paint they have found came from the suspect's car. Although there are lots of different red cars, the red paint used by different car manufacturers usually has different combinations of chemicals in it. Forensic scientists can test the paint to find the chemicals in it, and may be able to match it up to a particular make or model of car.

Even the tiniest strand of hair or fiber can foil a criminal mastermind!

HOW TO CREATE A WILDLIFE PARADISE

Lots of people like watching birds, and encourage birds to come to their gardens by putting out food. But there are other ways that you can encourage birds and lots of other kinds of wildlife to come into your garden.

WHAT WILDLIFE NEEDS

Animals need food and somewhere to hide from predators. Many birds eat seeds, so you can tempt these birds to visit your garden by having plants that produce lots of seeds. However, other birds eat worms and insects, so you also need to encourage lots of other wildlife!

DIFFERENT ANIMALS

To a scientist, the word "animal" includes birds, fish, insects, and other groups of living things. Animals such as squirrels and cats are all mammals. Birds are animals with feathers. Snakes and lizards are

see for yourself

There are many ways you can attract wildlife into your garden. Leave some long grass in the lawn. This gives somewhere for insects and spiders to shelter and lay their eggs. Do not cut down plants as soon as they have finished flowering. The seeds that come after the flowers will provide food for birds.

Putting out nuts and seeds during the winter months will attract plenty of hungry birds.

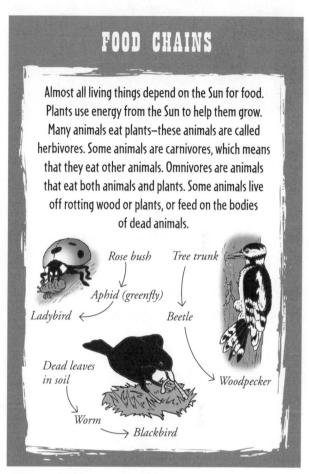

FOOD CHAINS

Almost all living things depend on the Sun for food. Plants use energy from the Sun to help them grow. Many animals eat plants–these animals are called herbivores. Some animals are carnivores, which means that they eat other animals. Omnivores are animals that eat both animals and plants. Some animals live off rotting wood or plants, or feed on the bodies of dead animals.

Rose bush

Tree trunk

Aphid (greenfly)

Ladybird

Beetle

Dead leaves in soil

Woodpecker

Worm → Blackbird

reptiles, and frogs and toads are amphibians. Smaller animals are divided into insects, worms, and many other groups.

CHOOSING PLANTS

You can encourage wildlife to come to your garden by choosing a collection of plants so that there are flowers for most of the year. These flowers will attract butterflies, bees, and other insects that feed off the pollen and nectar produced by the flowers. More insects will encourage birds that eat insects.

8 HOW TO CLIMB EVEREST

You take the last few steps very slowly, but at last you are there. The highest person in the world, on top of Mount Everest, 29,035 ft (8,850 m) high! But it has taken a lot of effort and training to get here. So what do you need to do to climb Mount Everest?

MOUNT EVEREST

Mount Everest is the highest mountain in the world. It is part of the Himalayan range of mountains in Asia. These run through Nepal and along the border between India and China. Everest has very steep sides, and it is covered in ice and snow all year round. There can be very strong winds and bad storms, and the weather is usually only good enough for climbers to go up it in April and May. Even then, the weather can change in an instant, making this peak very dangerous.

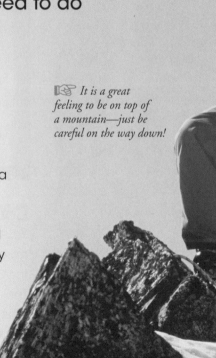

☞ It is a great feeling to be on top of a mountain—just be careful on the way down!

BEWARE!

Climbing mountains like Everest can be dangerous. On the way climbers have to walk along glaciers (like very slow-moving rivers of ice) that may have crevasses (deep gashes in the ice). Climbers use ladders and ropes to cross these crevasses. They may also have to dodge falling ice and rocks, climb almost vertical faces, and survive the weather and the lack of oxygen in the air. It is also very cold—you can find out more about clothing to keep you warm on page 123.

SETTING UP CAMPS

Many mountains in Europe and North America can be climbed in a single day. But Everest is too high and too far from roads and towns to do this. Climbers start from Base Camp at the bottom of the Khumbu Glacier. It then usually takes another three or four days, or sometimes even more, to get to the top. The climbers have to carry everything they will use during the long climb.

CLIMBING ON ICE

Ice is very hard and slippery, so climbers need special equipment. They use ropes to stop themselves falling if they slip. Hundreds of climbers attempt to get to the summit of Everest every year, so as soon as the weather is good enough some climbers set up fixed ropes. These stay on the mountain and climbers can clip their harnesses to the ropes.

The climber can pull up on ice axes. The pointed end sticks into the ice

Helmet to protect head against falling ice or rocks

Harness to attach the rope

Crampons have 12 spikes that stick into the ice

Stiff plastic boots are padded and waterproof to keep feet warm

GUIDES

Expeditions hire local guides and climbers to help them to carry all this equipment, including food and cooking gear. The tents and clothes are made from special lightweight but strong materials. Climbers choose their food carefully to give them lots of energy for climbing.

ALTITUDE SICKNESS

As you climb higher and higher up a mountain, the air gets "thinner." This means that each time you breathe a lungful of air, your body gets less oxygen out of it. Even the fittest climbers have to move more slowly than usual at high altitudes, and stop for rests, because their bodies cannot get enough oxygen. The lack of oxygen can also give climbers "altitude

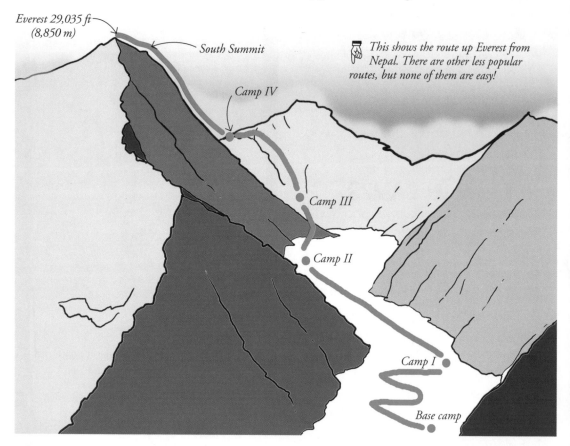

Everest 29,035 ft (8,850 m)

South Summit

Camp IV

Camp III

Camp II

Camp I

Base camp

This shows the route up Everest from Nepal. There are other less popular routes, but none of them are easy!

sickness"—they have headaches, feel sick, and cannot sleep properly.

TROUBLE BREATHING?

The high altitude can also cause more serious problems. Our bodies are full of liquids, mostly in the blood. At high altitude, liquid sometimes gets into the lungs and then climbers cough and cannot breathe properly. Sometimes, the liquid gets into the brain. Both of these conditions can cause the climber to die.

SHERPAS

The Sherpas are people who live in the Everest region. Many Sherpas are employed as guides for climbing expeditions. Because they live at high altitudes all the time, the Sherpas can cope with the conditions better than people who live at lower levels.

ACCLIMATIZING

People who normally live at low levels can gradually adapt to the high altitudes if they ascend slowly. A climber who takes two or three weeks to get from the valleys in Nepal up to the top of Everest will survive. If the same climber got a helicopter flight from the valley straight up to the summit, he would probably die! Your blood contains red blood cells that

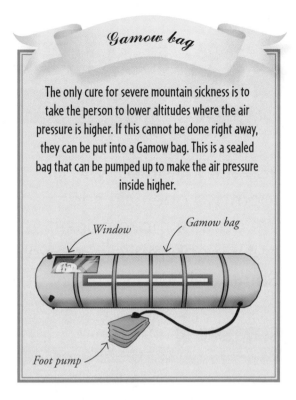

Gamow bag

The only cure for severe mountain sickness is to take the person to lower altitudes where the air pressure is higher. If this cannot be done right away, they can be put into a Gamow bag. This is a sealed bag that can be pumped up to make the air pressure inside higher.

Window

Gamow bag

Foot pump

carry oxygen around your body. If you gradually climb higher and higher your body can make more red blood cells, so your body gets more of the oxygen out of the air.

BOTTLED AIR

Climbers can also avoid altitude sickness by carrying bottles of oxygen to breathe through a face mask. This allows them to climb faster, but the bottles of oxygen are heavy and they all have to be carried up the mountain.

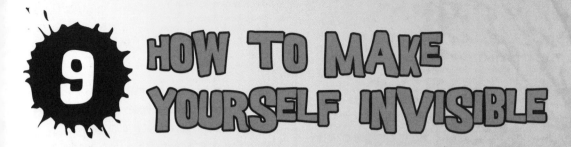

9 HOW TO MAKE YOURSELF INVISIBLE

You are invisible if you are in a completely dark room. No one can see you if there is no light! We cannot make ourselves invisible in daylight, but we can make ourselves very difficult to see. Some animals are really good at doing this.

BLENDING IN

It is easy to see things when they are a different color from the things behind them. The soldier in the photo on the right is harder to see because he is wearing clothes that match the colors and patterns of the forest. He would be even better camouflaged if he stuck ferns or bits of grass in his hat and clothing. These would help to disguise his shape.

CAMOUFLAGE

The best kinds of camouflage work to hide the animal or person from all directions. Many animals have colors or patterns that make them more difficult to see.

Predators that kill and eat other animals are sometimes camouflaged so they can creep up on their prey without being seen. For example, tigers have stripes so they can hide among the stems of tall grasses. Other animals are camouflaged to try to hide from their predators.

see for yourself

You can test camouflage on your friends. Take four balls, and camouflage two by shading them or sticking bits of grass or twigs to them. Put them in a flower bed in your garden, and challenge a friend to find them. See how easily they find the uncamouflaged ones compared to the camouflaged ones.

☞ *Now you see him, now you don't. Soldiers have to make sure their camouflage matches their surroundings or they might be too easy to spot!*

ANIMALS BLENDING IN

Most animal camouflage works only in one kind of surrounding. The stripes on a tiger help it to hide in forests and jungles, because the stripes blend in with the stalks of plants. But when the tiger is out in the open, the stripes do not help.

Some animals change the color of their fur or feathers twice a year. Animals that live in places where there is a lot of snow in the winter often grow white fur or feathers for the winter. This white fur is very easy to see in the summer, when the snow has gone, so they grow a new, darker coat in the spring.

You can change the color of your skin quite quickly—you go red in the face if you are embarrassed or if you are very hot. Some animals can do much better than this. The photo above shows a fish called a flounder. It has changed the

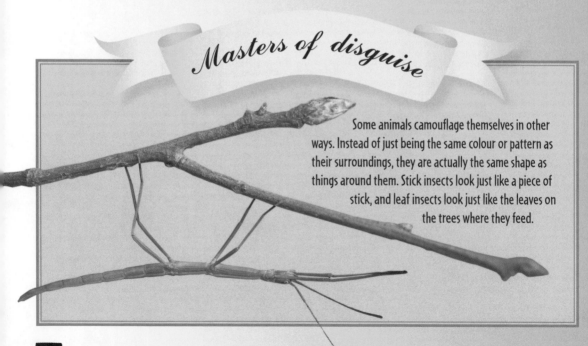

Masters of disguise

Some animals camouflage themselves in other ways. Instead of just being the same colour or pattern as their surroundings, they are actually the same shape as things around them. Stick insects look just like a piece of stick, and leaf insects look just like the leaves on the trees where they feed.

color and pattern of its skin to match the seabed beneath it. Cuttlefish and chameleons can also change the color of their skin to match their surroundings.

THE OPPOSITE OF CAMOUFLAGE

Some animals are very bright and colorful. For example, wasps and bees have black and yellow stripes that make them quite easy to see. Poison dart frogs are bright blue or have black and yellow blotches and there are many other examples. These animals are bright and easy to see as a warning to predators that they are poisonous, they taste horrible, or that they have a stinger. Predators avoid animals with these warning colors.

But some animals cheat! For example, hoverflies (below) look like wasps, but they do not have a stinger. They mimic the coloring of wasps so that predators will avoid them too, even though they are completely harmless.

Not all brightly colored animals use their colors to warn off predators. Some animals, particularly males, have bright colors to attract mates.

INVISIBLE VEHICLES

Military vehicles are painted in camouflage colors and patterns that make them harder to see. They are painted in colors to suit where they are being used. For example, vehicles used in the desert are painted a sandy color, those used in the snow are painted grey and white, while those used in places with lots of trees and grass are painted green.

It may soon be possible to make tanks or other vehicles more like flounders or cuttlefish. The tank would have cameras on one side, and the other side of the tank would have a display. The display would show the scenery that the cameras photographed. This method would disguise the tank only from people to one side of it, so it isn't really invisible.

Cameras take pictures of the scenery on this side of the tank

A screen on this side of the tank shows the image recorded by the camera

10 HOW TO LIVE TO BE 120

One way of living to be older than 120 years is to be born as a whale (the oldest whale we know about was more than 200 years old when it died) or a tortoise (more than 250 years). But if you want to stay as a human, what can you do to live a long time?

CHOOSE YOUR PARENTS

Unfortunately the best way of living a long time is just as impossible for you to do as choosing to be a different animal. You would have to choose parents who live a long time! We inherit lots of things from our parents, such as the shape of our faces and the color of our eyes. We can also inherit things such as how likely we are to suffer from heart disease. But as you have already been born, you cannot choose new parents!

HEALTHY LIFESTYLE

In some countries, diseases are the main cause of death. If you live in a country where there is plenty of food, good drains, and good health care, the things that are most likely to kill you are illnesses such as cancer or heart problems. You can reduce your risk of these by eating a healthy and varied diet and by getting enough exercise. You also need to eat the right amount of food for the amount of exercise you do. If you eat more than your body needs, you will put on weight.

You do not have to be thin to be healthy, but being very overweight is bad for your heart. Being too thin is also a problem.

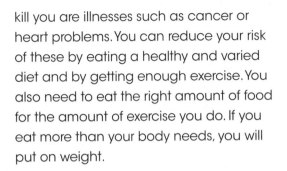

HEALTHY EATING

Having a healthy diet means eating the right kinds of food as well as not eating too much. The food triangle shows how much of each kind of food you should eat for a balanced diet.

☞ *You should eat less of the things at the top of the food pyramid (fatty foods, meat, and dairy) and more of the things at the bottom (cereals, pasta, and brown bread).*

☞ *If you eat a balanced diet and exercise regularly, you will enjoy life more and could even live to be 120—but you probably won't live as long as this tortoise.*

11 HOW TO EXPLORE A VOLCANO

Volcanoes can be dangerous things. A big eruption can kill many thousands of people. Scientists need to study volcanoes so they can work out when they might erupt, and give people warnings.

WHY VOLCANOES ERUPT

The ground beneath you is part of the thin outer layer that makes up the Earth's crust. Underneath the crust is the mantle, where the rocks are much hotter. Sometimes the rock in the mantle gets so hot that it melts. This molten rock pushes upwards through the mantle and crust, and bursts out at the surface. When it is inside the Earth, the molten rock is called magma and when it flows onto the surface it is called lava. The lava cools down and becomes solid. Lava cooling around a volcano gradually builds it up into a cone shape.

DEATH BY VOLCANO

Explosive volcanoes are the most dangerous. When these erupt, they shoot out ash and lava. The lava often cools and becomes solid while flying through the air, so if you are nearby you would see rocks falling around you. Sometimes a cloud of gas and dust runs down the side of a volcano. This "pyroclastic flow" can move at 435 mph (700 km/h)—which is far too fast for people to outrun. The gas is poisonous—but that's the least of your worries! The extreme heat or the flying rocks will probably kill you before the poison takes effect.

DIFFERENT KINDS OF VOLCANO

Not all magma is the same. Some magma is quite runny and just flows out of a volcano when it erupts. This kind of lava moves slowly enough for people to get out of the way, so it is not very dangerous. The volcanoes on the Hawaiian islands have this kind of lava. In some volcanoes the magma is much thicker and does not flow easily. Gases in the lava get trapped and the pressure builds up. Eventually the pressure is so high that the volcano explodes. Volcanoes made by sticky magma and lava are usually much steeper, such as Mount Fuji (below).

Volcanoes are hotter than the hottest kitchen oven. A "pyroclastic flow" can measure 1,830°F (1,000°C).

DANGEROUS MUD

Many volcanoes are covered in snow and ice because they are in cold parts of the world or because they are very high. The heat of the lava can melt a lot of ice very quickly. This can cause floods or a mudflow, called a "lahar." Lahars can be very deep and move very fast, especially if they flow down a valley. When Nevado del Ruiz in Columbia erupted in 1985, a lahar flowed over the town of Armero and killed more than 20,000 people.

This house was half-buried by a lava flow that poured out of Mount Etna on the Mediterranean island of Sicily.

PREDICTING ERUPTIONS

Almost all of the deaths caused by volcanoes could be prevented if people were warned when an eruption is about to happen. Scientists can tell when a volcano might be about to erupt by the magma moving inside it. The movement of huge amounts of molten rock deep in the volcano causes lots of very small earthquakes. These earthquakes can be detected by special instruments called seismometers. The magma gathering under a volcano also makes the volcano a little bit bigger. Scientists can put very accurate measuring instruments, including lasers and tiltmeters, at several different places on a volcano to measure this movement.

WARNING TIME

However, even with all these instruments, scientists can only say that a volcano *might* erupt soon. They cannot say exactly *when* it will erupt. Having a warning at the right time is very important. People do not want to leave their homes if they do not have to. If scientists say that a volcano is about to erupt but it does not, people will move back into the danger area. The next time the scientists warn them, they may refuse to leave.

see for yourself

Put a small amount of vinegar in a dish and stand a piece of limestone in it (it must be limestone, not any other kind of rock). Leave the dish for a week or two, adding a little more vinegar if the dish dries up. Eventually, crystals will grow out of the top that look just like a cloud of ash and dust from the top of an erupting volcano.

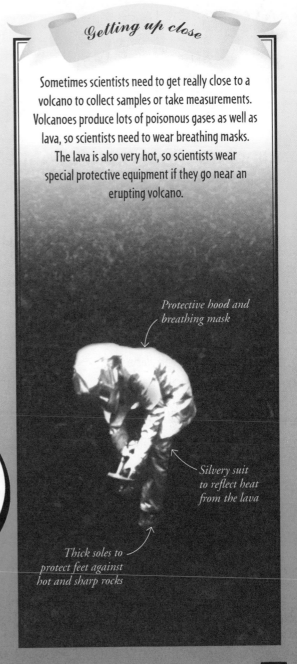

Getting up close

Sometimes scientists need to get really close to a volcano to collect samples or take measurements. Volcanoes produce lots of poisonous gases as well as lava, so scientists need to wear breathing masks. The lava is also very hot, so scientists wear special protective equipment if they go near an erupting volcano.

Protective hood and breathing mask

Silvery suit to reflect heat from the lava

Thick soles to protect feet against hot and sharp rocks

12 HOW TO FIND A DINOSAUR

Dinosaurs lived from about 230 to 65 million years ago. Although they are extinct, we know about dinosaurs because some of them turned into fossils. You can find some fossils yourself, although you are not likely to find a dinosaur!

FOSSIL FORMATION

Fossils are the shapes left by dead creatures' remains in rock. Most animals and plants do not become fossils because they are eaten by other animals. Animals or plants will only become a fossil if they are buried in mud or sand before something has a chance to eat them, and before they can rot. Gradually more mud or sand buries the remains. Over millions of years, heat and

pressure turn the mud or sand into rock, and the same thing happens to the remains to form a fossil. Some rocks get moved up to the surface again, revealing the fossil.

FINDING FOSSILS

The most common fossils are sea creatures with shells. This is because dead animals are most likely to become buried by sediments when they are in water, and because the hard shell does not get eaten and does not break up easily. Some limestone is almost entirely made of the shells of dead sea creatures.

Scientists can use fossils of dinosaurs to work out what they looked like when they were alive.

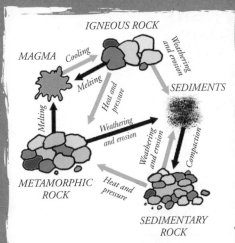

THE ROCK CYCLE

IGNEOUS ROCK

MAGMA   Cooling   Weathering and erosion

Melting   SEDIMENTS

Melting   Heat and pressure

Weathering and erosion   Weathering and erosion   Compaction

METAMORPHIC ROCK   Heat and pressure

SEDIMENTARY ROCK

When the Earth was first formed it was so hot that most of the rock was molten. When molten rock cools down it forms igneous rocks, such as basalt or granite. Wind, rain, and cold can break up rocks. Small pieces of rock can be carried away by the wind or by rivers. This is called erosion, and the bits of rock are called sediments.

Sediments often get washed into a lake or into the sea. More and more sediments build up, and they get squashed together to form sedimentary rocks, such as sandstone or limestone. Sometimes movements in the Earth bury rocks, and the heat and pressure underground changes them into metamorphic rocks.

WHERE TO LOOK FOR FOSSILS

Fossils form only when dead plants or animals are buried and the sediments that bury them turn into sedimentary rocks. Igneous rocks are formed from magma or lava (kinds of molten rock), and any animals that fell into the liquid rock would burn up right away. Metamorphic rocks are igneous or sedimentary rocks that have been changed by heat or pressure, and these changes usually destroy any fossils that were in the rocks. So there is no point in looking for fossils in places where the rocks are igneous or metamorphic! Sedimentary rocks include mudstone, sandstone, and limestone.

Trilobite

Fossils are formed within rocks. Professional fossil hunters, or scientists looking for fossils, may dig out large amounts of rock, but you will not be able to do that!

Ammonite

Mary Anning

Mary Anning is one of the most famous fossil hunters. She lived in Lyme Regis, in England, from 1799 to 1847. Her father made extra money for the family by selling fossils to visitors, and when he died Mary and her family carried on. Mary became famous as the person who discovered ichthyosaurs and plesiosaurs.

Ichthyosaur skeleton

Crinoid (sea lily)

Brachiopod

Old quarries can sometimes be good places to look for fossils, if the quarry is open to the public. NEVER go into a quarry if there are warning signs telling you to keep out.

RULES FOR FOSSIL HUNTING

Make sure you are safe! Do not go near loose cliffs and beware of the tide if you are fossil hunting on a beach. Check that you are allowed to collect fossils there— in some places the rocks are protected. If you find something very big, do not try to dig it out yourself. Contact your local museum or university for help. Scientists can get a lot of information from the way a fossil is buried, and you will destroy this information if you try to dig it out yourself. If there are lots of fossils, take only a few. Leave some for other fossil hunters to find.

he best places for amateurs to look for
ssils are places where rocks are being
roken up by other means. For example,
you live near a seashore with cliffs,
ou will know that the waves often knock
eces off the cliffs, or bits of cliff
metimes collapse. The fallen rocks are
od places to look for fossils—but never
right up to cliffs, and make sure the
e is out when you go.

13 HOW TO LIVE IN THE ARCTIC

The Arctic is cold and a lot of it is permanently covered in ice and snow. In some places the ice melts in the summer, and some plants grow, but they do not grow very fast. You need to be able to keep warm and to find food to survive in the Arctic.

KEEPING WARM

People living in very cold parts of the world have made clothes from animal skins for thousands of years. Arctic animals, such as polar bears, are adapted to the cold, and their fur keeps them warm even when the temperatures are well below the freezing point. The Inuit people used to hunt polar bears for food, using the skins to make warm clothing. Another important way of keeping warm is to have shelter. The traditional Inuit shelter was the igloo, made from blocks of ice. This might sound cold, but with only heat from the bodies of the people inside, the igloo can be as warm as your home!

GETTING FOOD

The Inuit were traditionally "hunter-gatherers." Hunter-gatherers do not have farms to grow their food, but eat what they can catch and kill, or what they can find growing. Some of the Sami people were nomadic herders; they used reindeer for food and skins, and followed the reindeer as they migrated. Some Sami lived south of the Arctic where it was a little warmer, and grew crops for food. The Inuit hunted seals, walruses, and polar bears, and caught fish and birds. They also gathered birds' eggs, roots, and some plants, such as seaweed.

You'll need to drill through the ice if you want to catch any fish for your supper.

Different groups of people have lived in the Arctic for centuries. The best known are the Inuit in northern Canada, Alaska, and Greenland, and the Sami in Norway. Traditionally, these people used the animals and the few plants that live and grow in the Arctic.

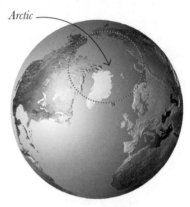

Arctic

The Arctic is the part of the Earth near the North Pole. The weather is very cold here, and it is dark for up to six months of the year (you can find out more about this on page 124). The Arctic includes Greenland, parts of Alaska and Canada, and parts of Russia and Norway.

This kind of diet has a lot of protein and is high in fat, but it does not have many carbohydrates (you can find out more about food on page 39). Eating like the Inuit would be very unhealthy for most of us, but the Inuit have adapted to stay healthy on their diet.

FIRE AND COOKING

There are no trees in the Arctic, so there is no wood to burn. Occasionally driftwood arrives from the sea, and people can collect plants, such as moss, and dry them to use as fuel. Animal droppings can also be dried and used as fuel. In the past the Inuit ate most of their food raw, so they did not need fires for cooking. The animals they caught for food all have thick layers of blubber (fat) under the skin, and this could be melted down and used as fuel for lamps.

LIVING AT THE POLES

No one lives permanently at the North Pole. There is no land there, and the ice is floating on the sea beneath. The part of the Earth near the South Pole is called the Antarctic. There is a large continent

Arctic animals

Polar bears live in the Arctic. They spend most of the winter in dens dug in the snow. They sleep a lot of the time, so their bodies do not use much energy. A mother polar bear can lose up to 440 lb (200 kg) in body weight over the winter. Polar bears hunt seals for food. Seals and walruses live in the sea and eat fish. They must to come to the surface to breathe. They need to be on ice or on land to give birth and while their babies are young, like this baby harp seal.

All Arctic animals are adapted to the cold by having thick layers of fat under their skin. This is a good insulator, and helps to stop body heat escaping.

around the South Pole, but it is permanently covered by ice that can be more than 2.5 miles (4 km) thick in places. There are no native people that live in the Antarctic. But there is a scientific station owned by the USA at the South Pole, and many other research stations.

DAY AND NIGHT

At the poles it is dark for six months of the year. About 50 people stay at the South Pole station over the winter when it is dark and extremely cold. But more go there in the Antarctic summer to carry out scientific research.

☞ *Scientists at this scientific research station in Antarctica study the atmosphere looking for the effects of climate change in the region.*

14 HOW TO FIND A METEORITE

If you have been outdoors on a clear night, you may have been lucky enough to see a streak of light across the sky. This is a meteor, sometimes called a "shooting star" (even though it has nothing to do with stars).

see for yourself

The best time to watch for meteors is around August 12 each year, when the Perseid meteor shower happens, or around November 17, when the Leonid meteor shower happens. The exact times vary each year, but you can find out exactly when to watch using the internet.

WHAT ARE METEORS AND METEORITES?

Meteors are small pieces of rock from space that fall into the Earth's atmosphere. They are moving very fast, and heat up as they pass through the air, becoming so hot they glow. We can see the streaks of light made by meteors as they travel across the sky. Most meteors burn up in the atmosphere. However, some of them are big enough to survive, and then what is left of the lump of rock hits the ground. When the rock hits the ground it is called a meteorite.

HOW TO FIND METEORITES

You are likely to find a meteorite only if you are lucky enough to see one land (and also lucky enough not to be hit by it!). This is because after it has landed and cooled down, a meteorite looks just like any

Streaks of light aren't invaders from another planet. They're just small rocks burning up in the atmosphere.

WHAT HAPPENS WHEN A BIG METEORITE HITS THE EARTH?

Most meteorites are small enough to fit in your hand. Every so often a larger meteorite hits the Earth. The Barringer Crater is in Arizona, USA. It was made by a meteorite about 164 ft (50 m) across that hit the Earth about 50,000 years ago.

Perhaps the most famous object to hit the Earth is the meteorite that landed 65 million years ago. There is no sign of the meteorite itself, but scientists have detected the crater it made in Mexico, which is about 112 miles (180 km) wide. The crater is now partly under the sea, and buried under layers of rock. The effects of this impact may be why the dinosaurs became extinct.

other lump of rock that might be lying around.

The best place to look for meteorites is in the Arctic or Antarctic. The rocks there are buried deep beneath the snow and ice, so any loose pieces of rock on the surface are likely to have come from space. Scientists collect meteorites because they can give us clues about how the solar system formed

15 HOW TO SURVIVE A LIGHTNING STRIKE

Every year there are about 16 million storms in the world that produce lightning. A lightning strike can damage buildings and hurt or even kill people. So how can you stay safe in a lightning storm?

WHAT CAUSES LIGHTNING AND THUNDER?

Have you ever heard and felt your hair crackle when you pull a shirt over your head, or got a small shock when you touch a door handle or car door? These effects are caused by static electricity. Rubbing certain materials can charge them up with static electricity. If a big enough charge builds up, the electricity can jump across gaps with a spark.

Lightning is a spark caused by static electricity that has built up in storm clouds. The lightning suddenly heats up the air through which it travels, causing thunder.

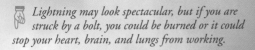
Lightning may look spectacular, but if you are struck by a bolt, you could be burned or it could stop your heart, brain, and lungs from working.

HOW FAR AWAY IS THE STORM?

You usually see the lightning before you hear the thunder because light travels much faster than sound. You can work out how far away a storm is by counting the number of seconds between seeing the lightning and hearing the thunder. Divide the number of seconds by five, and that is the distance of the storm in miles.

WHAT IF IT STRIKES A HOUSE?

Lightning transfers a lot of energy very quickly. This can damage buildings and things such as trees. Lightning travels through electrical wires easily, including the wires inside a house. This can cause too much electricity to flow through gadgets, such as computers, which damages them.

WHAT IF IT STRIKES A PERSON OR PET?

If lightning strikes a person or an animal it can cause severe burns. If it flows through your head or past your chest, it can damage your brain or make your heart and lungs stop working. And if your heart and lungs do not start to work again, or there is no one around to help you, you will die.

PROTECTING AGAINST LIGHTNING

Many buildings are protected by a lightning conductor. This is a metal spike that sticks above the highest point of the building and is connected to a wire that runs down into the ground. If lightning strikes the building, it is most likely to hit the conductor. It is easier for the electricity from the lightning to travel through the wire than through the building, so the wire takes it all safely down into the ground. Another way of protecting things against lightning is to use a "Faraday cage." If something is surrounded by metal wires, lightning will travel around the object in the metal instead of going through it.

WHAT TO DO IN A STORM

The safest place to be in a thunderstorm is inside a building. Stay away from taps and electrical devices. These are all connected to the outside by metal pipes or wires. Lightning striking the house could travel through this metal and strike you.

Being inside a car is the next best place to be in a storm. The car makes a metal cage around you, like a Faraday cage. If lightning strikes the car, the electricity will flow around the metal instead of through you. Keep the windows of the car closed, and do not touch the doors or other parts of the outside of the car.

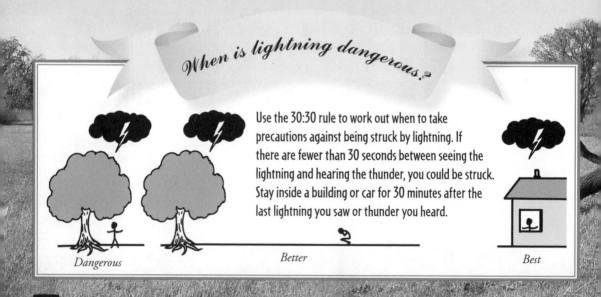

When is lightning dangerous?

Use the 30:30 rule to work out when to take precautions against being struck by lightning. If there are fewer than 30 seconds between seeing the lightning and hearing the thunder, you could be struck. Stay inside a building or car for 30 minutes after the last lightning you saw or thunder you heard.

Dangerous   *Better*   *Best*

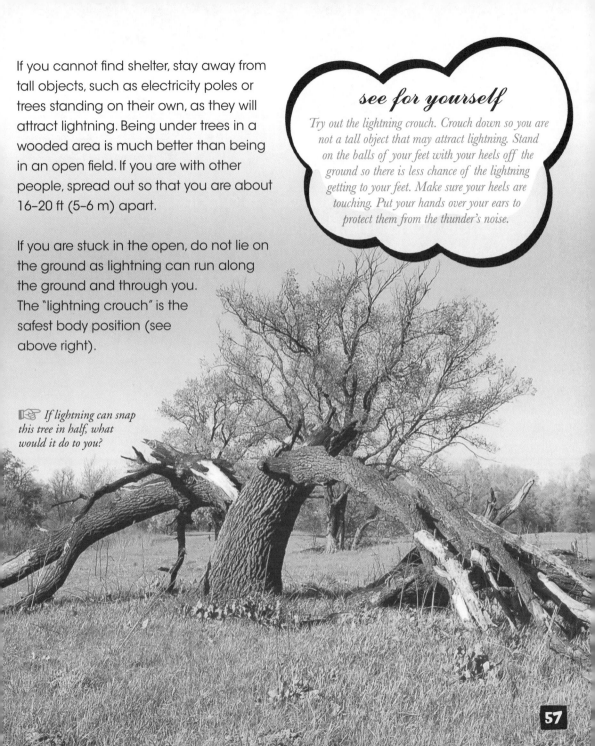

If you cannot find shelter, stay away from tall objects, such as electricity poles or trees standing on their own, as they will attract lightning. Being under trees in a wooded area is much better than being in an open field. If you are with other people, spread out so that you are about 16–20 ft (5–6 m) apart.

If you are stuck in the open, do not lie on the ground as lightning can run along the ground and through you. The "lightning crouch" is the safest body position (see above right).

☞ *If lightning can snap this tree in half, what would it do to you?*

see for yourself

Try out the lightning crouch. Crouch down so you are not a tall object that may attract lightning. Stand on the balls of your feet with your heels off the ground so there is less chance of the lightning getting to your feet. Make sure your heels are touching. Put your hands over your ears to protect them from the thunder's noise.

16 HOW TO DIVE TO THE BOTTOM OF THE OCEAN

Far beneath the ocean surface is a dark and strange world. The average depth of the oceans is 13,123 ft (4,000 m), and the deepest part is more than 36,089 ft (11,000 m) deep! What is it like down there, and how can we get there?

WHAT IS THE DEEP OCEAN LIKE?

On land, the air around you is pressing on you all over. You do not notice this pressure because it happens all the time. If you dive under the sea, the water presses on you even more. By the time you have gone down only 33 ft (10 m) the pressure on you has doubled. As you go deeper and deeper under the sea, the pressure increases even more. In the deepest part of the ocean, the pressure would be more than 1,000 times greater.

COLD

The water is also cold and dark. Even on the sunniest day, light cannot get through more than 656 ft (200 m) of water. If you go deeper than this you will need to have lights with you to see things. The temperature gets colder until it is almost freezing, but it does not get any colder than this. The deep oceans do not freeze.

There are some strange creatures living in the deep oceans—and some of them would like to make a meal of you!

THE BENDS

The first people to go diving often had very bad pains in their arms and legs, which made them bend over with pain. This condition was called "the bends." Sometimes the divers were permanently injured or even died. Scientists eventually found that this happened because when they breathed air at high pressure underwater, some of the gas dissolved in their blood. When they came up out of the water the pressure suddenly got less and the gases made bubbles in their joints. You can see this for yourself if you shake a bottle of a fizzy drink. Gas dissolved in the drink makes it fizzy. When you take the top off the bottle the pressure suddenly gets less and you can see lots of bubbles forming.

Divers can avoid the bends by coming up very slowly. But they need to make sure they have enough bottles of air with them! A diver who spends three hours at 66 ft (20 m) deep needs to spend a whole hour coming up slowly to avoid the bends. That means he or she needs to make sure that there is enough air for at least four hours.

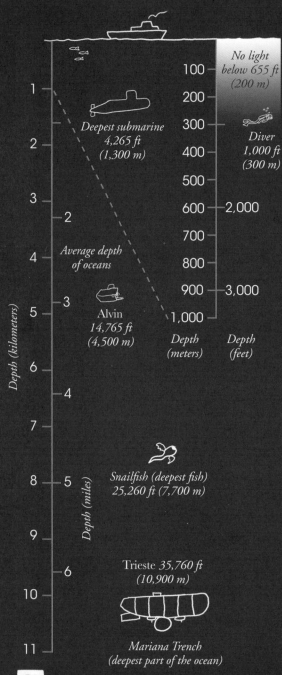

No light
below 655 ft
(200 m)

100
200
300

Diver
1,000 ft
(300 m)

400
500
600 — 2,000
700

Deepest submarine
4,265 ft
(1,300 m)

1
2
3
4
5
6
7
8
9
10
11

Depth (kilometers)

Average depth
of oceans

2

3
Alvin
14,765 ft
(4,500 m)

900 — 3,000
1,000

Depth
(meters)

Depth
(feet)

4

5

6

Depth (miles)

Snailfish (deepest fish)
25,260 ft (7,700 m)

Trieste 35,760 ft
(10,900 m)

Mariana Trench
(deepest part of the ocean)

DEEP-SEA LIGHT

Even though sunlight cannot get down to the deep oceans, there is still some light. Some fish make their own light. Anglerfish have a small prominence, called a "lure" on their heads. The lure contains a small light, which the anglerfish waves about just in front of its mouth. The light attracts other fish, which the anglerfish eats!

Black smokers are home to some unusual underwater wildlife, including tube worms.

BLACK SMOKERS

But the most famous discovery made by scientists was the existence of "black smokers." These are chimneys where very hot water—at more than 752°F (400°C) —comes out of the sea floor. Bacteria live

Small propellers to move the submersible around

Part of the sphere that protects the crew from the pressure

Robotic arms to take samples from the seabed

This part contains batteries to work the propellers and the lights

Basket for carrying samples up to the surface

You need a submarine to go deeper than a few hundred yards. But even submarines can only go 4,265 ft (1,300 m) below the surface. To go deeper than this you need a specially designed submersible. This has a very strong capsule inside it that can withstand the great pressures in the deep oceans. In 1960, one submersible went almost to the bottom of the Mariana Trench, the deepest part of the oceans. No humans have been as deep as that since. Other submersibles are used by scientists to explore the oceans. They are fitted with robotic arms that can take samples of animals or rocks and bring them to the surface.

off some of the chemicals dissolved in this water, and other organisms live off the bacteria. This kind of "community" of living things is very unusual. Unlike all other living things on the planet, these creatures do not depend on the Sun for energy. You can find out more about food chains that do depend on the Sun on page 29.

see for yourself

You can feel water pressure for yourself with a bowl of water and a plastic or rubber glove (a thin glove is best). Put on the glove and put your hand into the water, without letting any water get into the glove. You should be able to feel the water pressing on your hand from all directions.

HOW TO LOOK FOR OTHER PLANETS

Our solar system has eight planets that orbit around the Sun. Before the invention of telescopes, people could see Mercury, Venus, Mars, Jupiter, and Saturn with the naked eye. So how were the other planets found, and do other stars have planets orbiting around them?

SPOTTING PLANETS

The word "planet" comes from a Greek word that means wanderer. If you look at the stars you will see that they are always in the same pattern. Planets do not stay in the same place in the sky, but seem to move against the fixed pattern of the stars. You cannot see this movement by looking at the planet, but if you look at the same patch of sky several nights in a row you should see that the planet is moving.

DISCOVERING PLANETS

Saturn is the most distant planet from the Sun that can be seen with the naked eye. Uranus and Neptune were discovered using telescopes. Telescopes also helped astronomers to discover other things in the solar system, such as comets and moons.

Galileo Galilei was one of the first people to use a telescope. In 1610, he discovered that ours was not the only

Venus is often easy to spot. As it is closer to the Sun than the Earth, it is only visible around sunrise and sunset. It is bright because it is covered in clouds so it reflects a lot of light. If you see one bright object near the horizon when the sky is still light, it is probably Venus. Use the internet to find a star map for where you live, to help you look for the other planets.

Probes sent to the distant planets, such as Jupiter, have discovered new moons and planetary rings.

planet with moons, when he saw four small points of light near Jupiter. Today, we know that nearly all the planets have moons—and that Jupiter has more than 60! Galileo also discovered that our Moon has mountains and craters. Until then, no one knew what made the patterns on the Moon.

MODERN TELESCOPES

People have been working on telescopes ever since, making them more and more powerful. Today the biggest telescopes are put on mountain tops, so they are above the clouds and above a lot of the dust and pollution in the air. Because they are much bigger they produce more magnification, but they also collect more light. This is important when you want to look at objects such as very dim, distant stars. There are also telescopes in space, which can get an even clearer view.

EXTRASOLAR PLANETS

An extrasolar planet is a planet that is orbiting around a star other than the Sun. The stars are far away, and planets are much smaller than stars. Stars produce their own light and planets do not, so the

High above the clouds, this telescope has a crystal clear view of the night sky.

The telescope that Galileo used was a refracting telescope that used lenses to magnify objects. The bigger the lenses, and the longer the telescope, the better magnification you get. But lenses don't keep their shape very well when they are very big, and they also produce colored fringes around the things you are looking at.

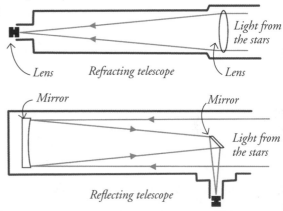

Light from the stars

Lens   *Refracting telescope*   Lens

Mirror   Mirror

Light from the stars

Reflecting telescope

In 1668, Isaac Newton built the first reflecting telescope. Reflecting telescopes use a large, curved mirror to collect light and produce a magnified image. It is easier to support a large mirror, because the light does not have to go through it. All the big modern astronomical telescopes are reflecting telescopes.

star is also very much brighter than any planets that are orbiting it. This makes it almost impossible to see extrasolar planets using a telescope. Astronomers have to use other methods to find them.

One way is to detect the "wobble" in the star that the planet makes as it moves around. Astronomers can make very careful measurements of the light coming from a star, and work out if it is moving towards or away from us. If the amount of movement changes with a regular pattern, there must be something near the star making it wobble. In 1995, the first extrasolar planet to be discovered was found this way.

BRIGHTER AND DIMMER

Other ways include measuring the brightness of a star very accurately. When a planet goes around a star, it will be between the star and the Earth some of the time, and will block out some of the light. This will make the star appear to be very slightly dimmer.

18 HOW TO SURVIVE A LONG FALL

During the Second World War, Nicholas Alkemade was in a plane when it was shot and caught fire. Unfortunately, his parachute was burning and damaged, so he decided to jump without it. He fell about 18,000 ft (5,500 m), but survived with only a sprained leg. So how did he survive?

FALLING AND STOPPING

The fall itself does not hurt and does not kill you. It is suddenly stopping when you hit the ground that does the damage! If you can slow down instead of stopping suddenly, the forces on you will be smaller and you are less likely to be injured.

When Nicholas Alkemade finally reached the ground, he fell through the branches of pine trees, which slowed him down a little bit. He then fell into deep snow, which also helped to slow him down instead of stopping very suddenly.

PARACHUTES

The first successful parachute jump was made in 1617, when Faust Vrancic jumped off a tower in Venice. The parachute he used was made from cloth stretched on a wooden frame. The first jump from a plane was made in 1911. This parachute was more like modern ones, being made of cloth with no rigid frame.

☞ *Modern parachutists carry altimeters on their wrists so they know when to open their parachutes.*

Today parachutes are made of light nylon and can be packed up very small.

PARACHUTES IN WAR

In the First World War, men in observation balloons were given parachutes so that they could escape safely if their balloon was shot and caught fire. However, pilots were not given parachutes because the government thought that having a parachute would encourage them to jump too soon if they were in danger. So if their airplane was badly damaged, they had no way of escaping. Today, the pilots of all fighter aircraft have parachutes as part of their ejection seat.

Parachutes are also used to drop soldiers into places they cannot reach by road, and to drop supplies in disaster areas.

AIR RESISTANCE

Parachutes slow a person's fall by creating air resistance. As the person is pulled down by the force of gravity, air forces the parachute to open out to cover a large area. This large area traps air beneath it, creating a great deal of air resistance. This acts against the force of gravity to slow the descent.

Air resistance

Force of gravity

Different kinds of parachute

Round parachutes produce a lot of air resistance. This force slows down the parachutist so he or she does not fall too fast. There is usually a hole in the middle of the parachute to let some air out. Without this hole air has to escape around the edges of the parachute, and this makes it swing from side to side. Round parachutes cannot be steered, so parachutists just have to land where the wind blows them.

Experienced skydivers use ram-air parachutes. These have hollow sections inside that fill with air when the parachute is used, giving the parachute a similar shape to the wing of an airplane. These parachutes actually fly like gliders. You can find out more about how wings work on page 119.

LANDING

If you fly a ram-air parachute properly, the landing can feel just like stepping off the bottom step of a staircase. But if you get it wrong, or if you are using a round parachute, the landing is more like jumping off a table. Parachutists make their landing softer by rolling when they land. When they roll, their feet touch the ground first, then their legs, then their back. This means they slow down gradually instead of stopping suddenly.

 While there is always a risk in parachuting, rolling helps to soften your landing.

SKYDIVING AND BASE JUMPING

For skydivers, the fun is in the free-fall part of the jump, before they open their parachutes. A skydiver can fall at up to 125 mph (200 km/h), before opening his or her parachute. Skydivers usually wear two parachutes. The second one is a reserve parachute that they will use if the first one goes wrong.

BASE jumping, where people jump off solid objects, is another parachute sport. BASE stands for Buildings, Antennae (such as telephone masts), Spans (bridges), and Earth (cliffs). This sport is even more dangerous than skydiving because there is a chance that the jumper can be blown into the solid object, and also because the landing areas may make a safe landing difficult.

see for yourself

One of the best examples of parachutes in nature is the dandelion plant: it uses special parachutes to disperse its seeds. The lightweight, fluffy part of the seed gets caught by the wind and acts like a parachute, carrying the seeds for long distances.

19 HOW TO BEAT A COLD

Nearly everyone has had a cold at some time. A bad cold makes you feel awful, with a runny, sore nose, sore throat, and often a cough, too. So if you catch a cold, how can you fight it?

DISEASES AND MICRO-ORGANISMS

Many diseases are caused by tiny micro-organisms called bacteria. These are so small that they can be seen only with a microscope. There are millions of different kinds of bacteria, and most of them are harmless. However some bacteria cause illnesses: *E. coli* and *Salmonella* cause food poisoning, some bacteria cause pneumonia, and *Yersinia pestis* causes the plague. However, many illnesses are caused by viruses, which are

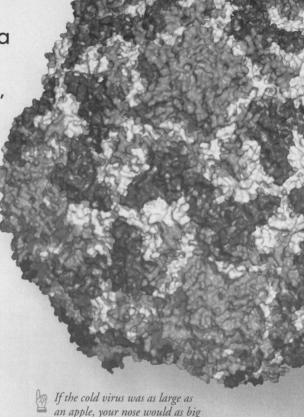

☞ *If the cold virus was as large as an apple, your nose would as big as the U.S. state of New Jersey.*

even smaller than bacteria. Viruses cause the common cold as well as other diseases, such as measles and stomach problems.

SPREADING DISEASES

Bacteria and viruses can spread in many different ways. Some spread through drinking water or in your food, and some get into your body through cuts or open sores. The viruses that cause colds are spread through the air.

If you have a cold, there will be some cold virus in the drops of liquid you spray out when you sneeze or cough. The virus could be breathed in by other people, and they will then catch your cold. The virus can also spread if it gets on something such as a door handle. If someone touches the door handle, and then touches his or her mouth, nose, or eyes, the virus can get into his or her body.

HOW TO STOP A COLD

If someone near you has a cold, ask him or her to use a handkerchief or tissue when sneezing or coughing. People with colds should try to catch all the droplets they sneeze out in a tissue, and then put the tissue in the garbage. If you get a cold, you should do the same so that you do not spread the cold!

FIGHTING A COLD

Your body tries to protect you from bacteria and viruses that may harm it. Special cells in your blood try to kill the bacteria and viruses. The symptoms of the cold (the runny nose, the cough, and so on) are caused by your body trying to fight the virus! There is no cure for the common cold. If you get a cold, you will feel better in about a week when your body has fought off the virus. Some people ask their doctor for medicines called antibiotics when they have a cold. Antibiotics kill only bacteria, they do not kill viruses, so they will not cure a cold.

Wash your hands often, and always wash them just before you eat food. If people around you have colds, you should try not to touch your mouth, nose, and eyes.

20 HOW TO MAKE IT RAIN

It might be a nuisance if it rains when you want to go for a picnic, but we need rain. Rain provides us with drinking water, and farmers need rain so their crops can grow. So why does it rain in some places and not in others, and can we make it rain?

MAKING IT RAIN

Clouds are tiny drops of water floating in the air. In some clouds, the drops of water join up to make bigger drops, and then these drops fall as rain. But sometimes the clouds just blow over without raining. If this happens, airplanes can fly over the clouds and drop chemicals into them. The chemicals help the droplets to join up to make drops that are big enough to fall as rain. But this method only works if the clouds are in the sky to start with.

The amount of rain is measured by the depth of the water inside a rain gauge. You can make your own rain gauge from an empty bottle and a ruler. Carefully cut the top off so that you have a bottle with an open top and straight sides. Use tape to fit the top upside down inside the bottle so it makes a funnel. Put your gauge in an open area away from trees and buildings. Measure the depth of the water that collects in the bottle after it rains.

Even plants that can survive in very dry conditions need some water to grow. Some deserts bloom after a rare rainstorm, when seeds in the soil suddenly start to grow.

THE WATER CYCLE

Clouds form as part of the water cycle. The water cycle depends on energy from the Sun. Warmth from the Sun makes some water in oceans, lakes, or rivers evaporate (turn into a gas). Water as a gas is invisible. The warmed air rises, and cools as it gets higher in the atmosphere. As the air cools, the water turns back into tiny drops of liquid and forms clouds. If the air cools even more the drops in the clouds form bigger drops and fall as rain. If it is cold enough, they fall as snow.

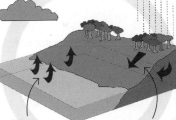

The water condenses and forms clouds

Rain or snow falls

Water evaporates

Water runs back into the sea or soaks into the ground

Rain that falls on land can soak into the ground, or it can run off into streams and rivers and eventually flow back into the sea. Some of the water in the ground is used by plants.

WHY ARE SOME PLACES WETTER THAN OTHERS?

The amount of rain that falls in a certain place depends on how close that place is to the sea and the direction that the winds usually blow. Parts of the world where the winds blow in from the sea usually have lots of rainfall. Rainfall is much less when there is a range of mountains between the place and the sea. In some countries the rainfall behind the mountains is so low that there is a desert. In the USA there is plenty of rain along the west coast of California, from wet winds blowing in from the Pacific Ocean. But the winds then blow across mountains, and to the east of the mountains there is desert.

MONSOON RAINS

There is a different pattern of rainfall in some parts of the world. In India, for example, there are heavy monsoon rains that last from June to September as the winds blow from the south, across the Indian Ocean. During the rest of the year the winds blow from the north, where there is only land and mountains. These winds are very dry, because they have not passed over water, and they do not form clouds and rain.

DESERTS

A desert is a place where very little rain falls and where there is not enough water for plants to grow. Some deserts, such as the Sahara Desert in Africa, are hot and covered in sand and rock. But not all deserts are hot and sandy. The Gobi in Asia is covered in rock, and the temperatures drop below freezing point in the winter. The Antarctic is also a desert even though it is

Winds usually blow in this direction

Sea

74

covered in snow and ice all year round. This is because all the water there is frozen and so plants cannot use it.

TURNING LAND TO DESERT

There are many reasons why an area may become a desert. For example, weather patterns may change so that fewer rain-bearing clouds blow over the area. Sometimes people can turn an area into a desert by cutting down trees. Trees have deep roots and can take a lot of water out of the ground. This water travels up inside the tree and most of it evaporates from the leaves. This water can then condense again to form clouds. If the trees are cut down, a lot of the water that would have gone into the trees and evaporated just runs away, and may wash soil away with it. All that's left behind is barren earth where nothing can grow and where no rain falls. So one way to make it rain in some places might be to plant more trees and provide them with water while they are growing!

There is no more moisture left in the air here, so there is hardly any rainfall. This area is in the "rain shadow" of the mountains.

The air is forced up over the mountains. It cools down as it rises, and the drops in the clouds grow bigger and fall as rain.

HOW TO MAKE YOURSELF SMARTER

Some people enter competitions to see how quickly they can remember the order of all 52 cards in a pack when they have been shuffled. But are these people really smart?

SMART OR NOT?

"Smart" can mean many different things. When you are talking about how people think, it could mean someone who knows a lot of facts. It could also mean someone who can solve problems or answer crossword puzzles quickly, or who always has a funny remark to make.

DIFFERENT BRAINS, DIFFERENT SKILLS

There are a few very lucky people who are good at lots of different things. Most of us are good at some things but not so good at others. For example, someone might be very good at mathematics but no good at drawing. Someone might be good at playing one or more musical instruments, but always makes mistakes when adding. Some people find it easy to learn many different languages, while others find it very difficult to learn just one more language.

BRAIN TRAINING

You can buy lots of different games and puzzles that say they "train your brain." Most of these games do make you better at the things you have to do in the game, such as matching up shapes, finding patterns of numbers, or working out sums. But they don't make you better at other things.

GET SMART!

If you want to be "smarter," make sure you get enough sleep and exercise and eat a healthy diet (read more about this on page 39). You should also do lots of different things that involve your brain, such as reading, doing puzzles, and solving crosswords. Try to make links between the different things you do. Just use your brain!

(read more about this on page 39)

see for yourself

How good is your memory? Ask a friend to put ten objects on a tray and cover them with a cloth. Remove the cloth for one minute and try to memorize the items. Cover them again, and write down what the objects were. Put ten different objects on the tray. This time make up a story with the objects in it. Can you remember more this time?

INTELLIGENCE TESTS

Many schools give their pupils tests to find out how "intelligent" they are. These tests ask you to work things out and may have questions like these below.

1 High is to low as top is to _____
2 Which is the odd one out? car, bus, bicycle, truck
3 What is the next number in this list? 1, 2, 4, 7, 11, ___
4 Which of these shapes is the odd one out?

A   B   C   D

Answers: 1) bottom, 2) bicycle, 3) 16, 4) D

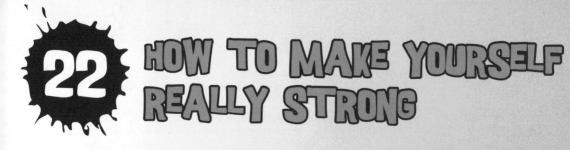

22 HOW TO MAKE YOURSELF REALLY STRONG

You use your muscles all the time. When people talk about being strong they are usually thinking about lifting heavy weights, but other sports need strong muscles, too. Sprinters have strong legs to help them run fast and shot-putters need upper body strength to throw their shot as far as possible.

MUSCLES AND JOINTS

Your skeleton gives your body shape—without it you would be a floppy heap! You can move because your skeleton has joints and muscles, which pull on the bones.

There are two kinds of movable joint in your skeleton. Some joints are hinge joints, for example, your elbows and knees. They can only move backwards and forwards. Other joints are ball-and-socket joints, such as your hips and your shoulders. These joints can move in lots of directions, and they can twist, too. Each joint has a set of muscles to move it in different directions. There are more than 600 different muscles in the human body. A lot of these are in your face and move your eyes and tongue—they let you smile, frown, and make lots of other expressions.

NO PAIN, NO GAIN!

Your muscles get stronger when you use them enough to damage them slightly. When your body repairs them, they get a little bit stronger. But "damage" here means that they hurt a bit when you finish exercising, and you may also feel sore the next day. If you want to develop your muscles without injury, you need to ask an expert to help you to work out a proper training program.

ANTAGONISTIC PAIRS

Muscles can only pull, they cannot push. This means that you need at least two muscles for every joint—one to move the joint in one direction and one to move it in the other direction. For example, if you want to bend your arm up, your biceps muscle contracts. You can feel your biceps muscle getting fatter as you bend your arm. When you straighten your arm again, the biceps muscle relaxes (stops pulling). The triceps muscle at the back of your arm contracts and pulls your arm straight again. Pairs of muscles like this are called "antagonistic pairs" because they pull in opposite directions to each other.

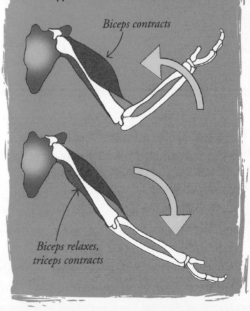

Biceps contracts

Biceps relaxes, triceps contracts

TRAINING

A good training program will include exercises that are hard enough to develop your muscles but not so hard that they harm your muscles permanently. The program will also include rest days, which allow your muscles to recover. You must take care not to exercise too much while you are still growing. You can develop strength for a sport by playing that sport, but this often develops one set of muscles more than others. It is a good idea to do some training in a different sport, so that all your muscles get stronger. This is called cross-training. For example, if you play tennis, you could cycle or swim, too. For many sports you also need to do some endurance training, such as jogging. Having good endurance means that you can exercise for a long time.

Weight training builds muscle too, but you need to be old enough to do it—you will need expert supervision!

Aerobic and anaerobic exercise

Muscles need energy to work. Energy comes from your food. Your digestive system turns food into glucose (a kind of sugar) in your blood, and some of this glucose is converted into other chemicals. Energy is released when glucose combines with oxygen in your muscles. The more you work your muscles, the more oxygen you need. This is why you breathe harder when you exercise.

Long-distance runners exercise "aerobically." This means that they can get all the oxygen they need from breathing. If you exercise very hard, for example sprinting as fast as you can, you cannot get oxygen into your body quickly enough. When this happens you are exercising "anaerobically." Different chemical reactions happen in your muscles to release energy. These reactions also make lactic acid. Lactic acid causes your muscles to "burn" when you are exercising. When you stop exercising, you need oxygen to get rid of this lactic acid. This is why you continue breathing hard after you have finished sprinting.

BODYBUILDING

Bodybuilders do a lot of weight training. They try to make their muscles bigger so that they can enter bodybuilding competitions. They also want their muscles to be "defined," which means that you can see where all the different muscles are under their skin. You have a layer of fat under your skin, which stops you seeing where the muscles are.

To improve their chances of winning, bodybuilders follow a special diet that is very high in protein. Protein helps to build up their muscles. They often go on a different diet before a competition to reduce the amount of fat under their skin, so you can see exactly where the muscles are.

☞ You can be fit and strong without having big muscles!

see for yourself

How long can you raise your arm before the lactic acid makes you want to stop? Find three different-sized books. Each one should be heavier than the next. With a friend keeping time, see how long you can hold each book above your head. The heavier the book and the more tired your muscles are, the harder this will be.

23 HOW TO THINK LIKE AN ANT

Most ants live in large colonies. They hunt for food, defend their colony, and keep it clean. Some ants are also farmers. How do they manage all this with such a tiny brain?

HOW ANTS LIVE

Ants are social insects. Most ant colonies have a queen ant. All she does is lay eggs. The other female ants are worker ants, who build and repair the nest, look for food, and take care of the eggs. Male ants only live long enough to mate with a queen ant so she can lay more eggs. The eggs hatch into larvae, which eventually change into ants.

An ant colony is organized using smells. If an ant is injured, it gives out a smelly chemical called a pheromone. The pheromone attracts other ants to it to fight off the danger. A dead ant gives out a different pheromone. If the dead ant is in the nest, this pheromone makes the other ants take the dead body away before it can cause disease. All the ants in a colony share a particular smell.

Ants live in highly organized colonies where they all work together to protect their colony and to find food.

Ants from a different colony will have a slightly different smell. Ants will attack any other ants in their colony that do not smell as though they belong there.

FINDING THEIR WAY AROUND

Some of the worker ants go out to look for food. If they find some food, they take it back to the nest. As they bring the food back, they leave a pheromone trail. Other ants can follow this trail to find the food and then find their way back to the nest.

Ants do not just use smells to find their way. Some kinds of ant find their way by remembering landmarks around them. Others can detect the direction of the Sun even on a cloudy day, and know how far they have traveled by the number of steps they have taken.

THINKING OR INSTINCT?

Do ants think at all? Probably not in the way that you can think. They carry out the tasks they need to do by instinct. You have some instincts yourself, such as blinking if something moves suddenly near your eyes. But you have learned most of the things you do, such as walking, eating with a knife and fork, and reading.

ANTS AND OTHER INSECTS

Aphids are small green insects that live on plants. They are sometimes called greenfly, and are considered a pest. When they feed on plants they produce a sweet liquid called honeydew. Some ants feed off this honeydew. The ants protect the aphids. If the ants move to a new colony, they may take some aphids with them.

Some kinds of caterpillar also produce honeydew. Ants take the caterpillars to places where they can feed, and then take them inside the nest at night so they can get the honeydew. But some caterpillars use the ants instead. The caterpillars give off pheromones that make them smell as if they belong to the colony. The ants let the caterpillars inside the colony and they eat the ant larvae.

DOGS AND SHEEP

Humans have a sense of smell, although we cannot smell nearly as well as dogs and other animals. Dogs use their sense

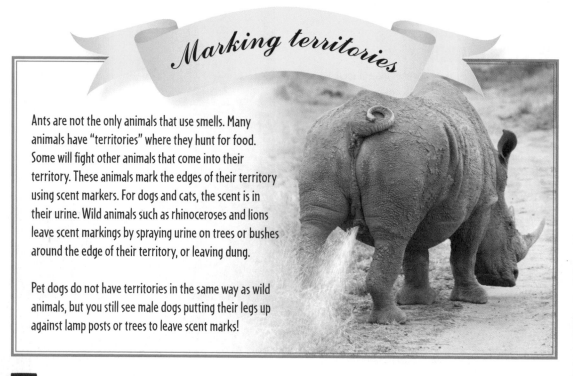

Marking territories

Ants are not the only animals that use smells. Many animals have "territories" where they hunt for food. Some will fight other animals that come into their territory. These animals mark the edges of their territory using scent markers. For dogs and cats, the scent is in their urine. Wild animals such as rhinoceroses and lions leave scent markings by spraying urine on trees or bushes around the edge of their territory, or leaving dung.

Pet dogs do not have territories in the same way as wild animals, but you still see male dogs putting their legs up against lamp posts or trees to leave scent marks!

of smell all the time. They even use it to identify other dogs. Dogs (and many other animals) have scent glands next to their bottoms. These produce a smelly chemical that other dogs can use to identify the dog. This is why dogs smell each others' bottoms when they meet!

Some scientists have tested humans to see if they can identify their family members by smell. They have found that mothers and new babies can recognize each others' smells.

Many animals recognize their own families by smell. Sheep farmers sometimes have a ewe (mother sheep) with a dead lamb, and may also have an orphaned lamb. The ewe with the dead lamb will not adopt the orphaned lamb unless it smells like her own lamb. Sheep farmers sometimes take the skin off the dead lamb and wrap it around the orphaned one so that it smells like the dead lamb. The ewe will then feed it and look after it because she thinks it is her own lamb.

Luckily humans do not use smell to identify each other! If we did, we would probably remove any natural smell by washing and using deodorant.

HOW TO SEE IN THE DARK

Most of the time at night there is a little light around to help us to see, perhaps from a street light or from the Moon. Our eyes adapt to let us see things in dim light, but how can we see things when it is completely dark?

ADAPTING TO THE DARK

When you go to bed and turn out the light, you probably cannot see anything around you. But after a few minutes you can see dim shapes. Your eyes have adapted to the dark.

The colored part of your eye is called the iris. The black circle in the middle is a hole in the iris, called the pupil, which lets light into your eye. When the light around you is bright, the pupil is small. This stops too much light getting into your eyes and damaging them. In dim light the size of your pupil increases to let more light into your eyes.

INFRARED

The light we see is a mixture of different colors. You can use a prism to spread these colors out into a spectrum (you can read more about this on page 139).

In 1800, William Herschel was doing an experiment with thermometers and a prism. He noticed that a thermometer in the red part of his spectrum was measuring a higher temperature than a thermometer in the blue part. He decided to see what would happen if he put the thermometer beyond the red light. This thermometer measured an even higher temperature! Herschel had discovered a kind of light that we call infrared (which means "below red").

We can detect infrared radiation using our skin —that is why sunlight feels warm. But this does not help us to use infrared to see things. We need to use a camera that can detect infrared light. Infrared cameras can be built into goggles to wear at night. They are not very useful for things such as reading road signs, because all of the sign is the same temperature. But they are useful for seeing warm things

You see things when light from them hits special cells on your retina (the back of your eye). There are two kinds of cells in our retina. The cone cells detect colors, but they can detect only fairly bright light. You also have a set of rod cells that can detect very dim light but cannot tell the difference between different colors. When it is dark, it is these rod cells, not the cone cells, that are allowing you to see. This is why you cannot see colors very well at night.

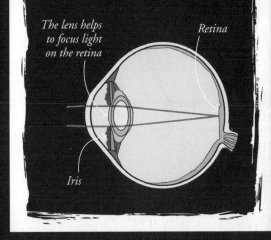

The lens helps to focus light on the retina

Retina

Iris

such as animals or cars (which get warm because of heat from their engines). Police use infrared cameras to track criminals at night.

An infrared image tells you the temperature of an object, or of different parts of it. The infrared photograph below shows a person. In this photograph, the coolest areas of the person are black while the warmest are white. You can see that the person's ears, neck, and face are the warmest parts, and the coldest are the nose and hair.

Coolest   *Warmest*

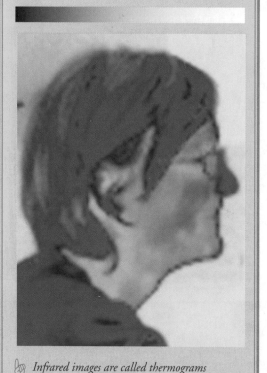

Infrared images are called thermograms —"thermo" means heat.

ANIMALS THAT SEE IN THE DARK

Some animals are much better than humans at seeing in dim light. Some animals, such as cats, and birds, such as owls, have a reflective layer at the backs of their eyes. Light going into their eyes passes through the layer of rods and cones, and some of this light is detected. Any light that has not been absorbed by the rods and cones is reflected and goes back past them again. This gives the eye a second chance to detect the light.

Have you ever seen a cat in the light from a car's headlights or in the beam of a flashlight? Their eyes seem to glow. This happens because the reflective layer at the back of their eyes is reflecting light back towards you.

Animals that hunt at night usually have very good night vision, but no animals can see in complete darkness. Most hunters also rely on smelling or hearing their prey.

SEEING WITH SOUND

Some animals "see" with their ears! Bats can safely fly around in the dark because they send out very high sounds (too high for humans to hear). These sounds are reflected by the things around the bat, and the bat hears the echoes. Their brains make an "image" of what is around them. This is called echolocation. Bats can fly at night without hitting each other or flying into trees, and they can even detect and catch tiny insects using echolocation.

Dolphins also use echolocation. Although they do not need to see in the dark, they do need to see underwater. Light does not travel very far under water because the water scatters it. Dolphins use their

see for yourself

To see infrared light, you can use a television remote control and a digital camera. Point the remote control at the camera and press a button on the remote control. As you press the button, look through the viewfinder of the digital camera. You should see a beam of infrared light.

echolocation to find prey in murky water, and can even use it to find objects just under the seabed.

Some dolphins are thought to use sound to stun their prey. This makes the prey much easier to catch and eat.

25 HOW TO FEED THE WORLD

The number of people on Earth is nearly seven billion, and by 2050 there could be up to ten billion people. More than a billion people do not get enough to eat. This problem is likely to get worse as the population increases. So what can we do to try to make sure everyone has enough?

GETTING FOOD TO WHERE IT IS WANTED

The farmers of the world grow enough food to feed everyone on the planet, but the food does not always get to the people who need it. In many parts of the world people are too poor to buy all the food they need. Even people who have land to farm cannot always grow enough food to survive. We could solve this problem by giving food to people who cannot afford it, but it would be better if each country could grow its own food.

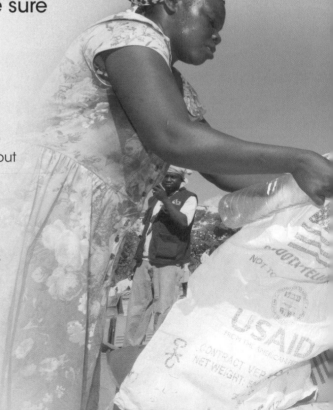

FERTILIZERS

Growing plants need light, water, and carbon dioxide from the air. They also need other chemicals, called nutrients. Plants get these nutrients from the soil. When the plants are harvested, the nutrients are removed as they are part of the plants. If a farmer is going to continue growing crops on a field, he or she needs to put back some nutrients.

One way of fertilizing a field is to allow animals to graze on the field because animal droppings contain some nutrients. However, the farmer cannot grow crops while the animals are grazing on the field. Artificial fertilizers are liquids or powders that farmers can spread on the fields to replace the nutrients. Poor farmers cannot always afford to buy fertilizers.

After Hurricane Ike destroyed parts of Haiti, food was sent to make sure the people there had enough to eat.

PEST AND DISEASE CONTROL

Plants can get diseases, just as humans can! Pests are insects or other organisms that eat the crops. Pests or diseases can destroy a farmer's entire crop. If they can afford it, farmers can buy chemicals (pesticides and fungicides) to protect the crops against diseases and pests, such as these slugs.

IRRIGATION

All crops need water to grow. In many parts of the world it rains only at certain times of the year, and sometimes the rains do not come at all. Crops can still grow in such places by using irrigation. Water from a nearby river or reservoir is sent to the fields in channels, or supplied by pipes and sprayed over the fields.

But there is not always a river nearby, and it costs a lot of money to build big dams. Farmers can get more water for their crops, or to use for drinking water, by harvesting rainwater. This means building large tanks to hold water collected from rooftops. They can also build small dams across gullies to stop the rain just running away and help it to soak into the ground instead.

IT'S MORE COMPLICATED THAN IT SOUNDS

It does not sound too difficult to grow lots of food, does it? You just need to provide water and fertilizer, and get rid of pests and diseases. But pesticides

These circles of crops are produced by irrigation systems. Irrigation can turn barren land into productive farmland.

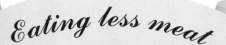

Many people like eating meat. Some meat comes from cows or sheep that graze on grass, but most of the meat we eat comes from intensively farmed animals. These animals are fed on grain or soya that has been grown especially to feed them. But it takes time for the cow or sheep to grow, and all that time it is using energy from its food. So by the time a piece of steak reaches our plate, about nine-tenths of the energy that was in the original grain has been used just to keep the animal alive. If we ate the grain directly, this energy would not be wasted. We could feed many more people on the same land if we ate less meat.

Nine-tenths of the energy in the grain that the cow eats is used to keep the cow alive.

Only one-tenth of the energy is turned into meat that we can eat.

can also kill useful insects. For example, many crop plants need insects to pollinate them before seeds or fruit will grow. Pesticides may get washed into the water supply and harm the people who drink the water. Fertilizer washed off fields into rivers can harm the fish and other things living in the river.

Even irrigation can have its problems. All water contains some dissolved salt. "Fresh" water does not contain much salt, but when the water is taken up by plants or evaporates from the soil, the salt gets left behind. Over many years, salt can build up in the soil. Most crops will not grow in salty soil.

26 HOW TO MAKE SWEET MUSIC

You can hear music almost everywhere you go—on radios or MP3 players, in shops, or at home from CDs or even on your computer. You can make music yourself, by singing. But how can you make other kinds of music?

DIFFERENT KINDS OF MUSICAL INSTRUMENT

Musical instruments make sounds in different ways. Percussion instruments make sounds when you hit or shake them. These percussion instruments include drums, cymbals, and xylophones.

Wind instruments make sounds when you blow into them. The group of wind instruments includes brass instruments, such as trumpets and trombones, and woodwind

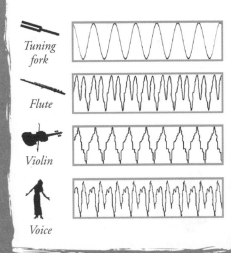

How many instruments can one person play? This one-man band is playing a combination of wind and string instruments.

instruments, such as flutes and clarinets.

Other instruments have strings. Violins are played by pulling a bow across the strings, or by plucking the strings. Guitars and harps are also played by plucking the strings. Pianos are also stringed instruments! Pressing the keys on a piano works a set of little hammers inside the instrument that hit strings.

The pitch of a musical note is how low or high it sounds. It depends on the frequency of the sound, which is how many sound waves arrive at your ears each second. High-frequency sounds have high pitches. The loudness of a sound depends on how big the sound waves are. You can play the same note on two different instruments, but the notes will not sound the same. This is because an instrument makes sounds of many frequencies together. The note is the main frequency. The combination of other frequencies is called the timber. Different instruments make different combinations of sounds, so they have different timbers.

Tuning fork

Flute

Violin

Voice

The strings of a guitar are different thicknesses, so they make different notes. The strings are wound around pegs at the top of the guitar so they can be tightened or loosened to adjust the sound. The tighter a string, the higher the note it makes. You can try this for yourself with an elastic band. Ask someone to hold the elastic band for you, stretched a little. Twang it, and then ask the person to stretch it more. Twang it again–it should sound higher.

Guitar players can make many different notes because they can press their fingers down on some of the strings. This changes the length of the part of the string that can vibrate and changes the note. The shorter they make a string, the higher the note.

Pegs for adjusting the tightness of the strings

The top string is the thickest, so it makes the lowest note

The hollow body helps to make the sound louder

The bottom string is the thinnest, so it makes the highest note

MAKING SOUNDS

Sounds are made when something vibrates. If you touch your throat while you sing, you can feel the vibrations made by your vocal cords as your lungs push air past them. Using a bow or hitting or plucking strings makes them vibrate, and the vibrating strings make the air near them vibrate. These vibrations travel out through the air and reach your ears.

A large orchestra combines instruments with a range of different pitches and timbres, including bassoons, oboes and flutes.

When you hit a drum, the drum skin vibrates. For brass instruments, musicians make a buzzing sound with their lips, and this makes the air inside the instrument vibrate. In woodwind instruments such as clarinets, the vibrations are made by blowing through reeds. In flutes and piccolos, the player blows across a hole in the instrument (just like blowing across the top of an empty bottle).

LARGE AND SMALL, HIGH AND LOW

Most musical instruments can make many different notes. The longer, thicker, or bigger the vibrating object is, the lower the note. You can see this on instruments such as xylophones or tubular bells—the long bars make the lowest notes. Big instruments, such as cellos or double basses, make much lower notes than violins, and saxophones make lower notes than piccolos.

see for yourself

Make a xylophone out of a set of drinking glasses. Set them up in a row and pour different amounts of water into each one. Tap the top of each glass with a spoon and see how different the notes are. The glass with the most water should make the lowest sound. Adjust the notes by changing the amount of water in the glasses.

HOW TO MAKE ELECTRICITY OUT OF SUNSHINE

We use electricity to do many things. Most of the electricity we use is made in power stations that burn coal or gas. But the Earth gets a huge amount of energy from the Sun, so it would be useful if we could use this energy to make electricity.

SOLAR CELLS

Solar cells can convert energy in sunlight directly into electricity. Solar cells like the ones in the photo are very useful for running small devices, or for charging up things like cell phones or other portable devices. Some people have solar cells on the roof of their house to produce electricity. There are even whole power stations that use solar cells, but these need to cover a very large area of land.

HOW A POWER STATION WORKS

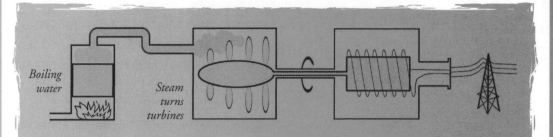

Boiling water

Steam turns turbines

If you spin a magnet inside a coil of wire, you make electricity flow in the wire. In power stations, fuel is burned to heat water and make steam. The steam makes huge fans, called turbines, spin around, and these spinning turbines spin the magnets. Nuclear power stations work in a similar way, except that nuclear energy is used to heat the water and make steam.

WHY BOTHER?

Why should we bother to make electricity from sunshine when there is oil and gas to use instead? One reason is convenience. Electricity from power stations is provided to users through a grid of wires across the country. Someone who is not connected to the grid cannot get electricity from power stations. People living in remote areas often use solar cells or wind turbines to generate their electricity. Solar cells are also useful for charging up small items without plugging them in.

Building solar power stations means that we will need to use less coal or gas to generate electricity, and this will help to reduce the amount of carbon dioxide we put into the air. (You can read why this is important on pages 144–147.)

Solar power means you can work anywhere you want to—even on a cloudy day!

SOLAR THERMAL POWER STATIONS

Solar thermal power stations have thousands of mirrors that are used to reflect heat and light from the Sun onto a central point. This can get very, very hot. The heat is used to turn water into steam. Power stations like this are built only in hot, sunny countries where there is plenty of sunshine. They do not work at night!

A DIFFERENT WAY OF USING THE SUN

Some ordinary power stations can burn biomass instead of coal or gas. Biomass is anything obtained from living things. For power stations, this can be wood chippings, stalks left after grain is harvested, or even crops grown especially to be used as fuel. Plants use energy from

A solar thermal power station. The mirrors are focusing light on the top of the tower.

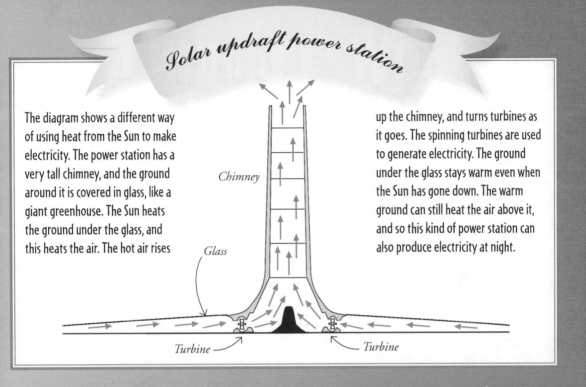

The diagram shows a different way of using heat from the Sun to make electricity. The power station has a very tall chimney, and the ground around it is covered in glass, like a giant greenhouse. The Sun heats the ground under the glass, and this heats the air. The hot air rises up the chimney, and turns turbines as it goes. The spinning turbines are used to generate electricity. The ground under the glass stays warm even when the Sun has gone down. The warm ground can still heat the air above it, and so this kind of power station can also produce electricity at night.

Chimney

Glass

Turbine

Turbine

the Sun to help them to grow, so in a way using biomass in a power station is making electricity from sunshine.

Even power stations that use coal or gas are using energy from sunshine. Coal and gas, together with oil, are all called fossil fuels. Coal is formed from the remains of plants that lived in swamps millions of years ago. Some of these plants got buried before they could rot away. They were buried by sand and mud, until they were several miles beneath the surface. Heat and pressure changed the chemicals into coal. Oil and gas were formed in a similar way beneath the sea.

The remains of dead organisms are trapped below layers of rock and transformed into oil and gas.

28 HOW TO HUNT WILD ANIMALS

Could you survive if you had to find your own food? You might be able to gather fruit or find other plants to eat, but for a balanced diet you would probably need to catch some animals or birds.

HUNTING

Many animals you could hunt would be bigger and more powerful than you. Smaller animals can probably run faster than you and birds can fly away. It would be very difficult to hunt animals for food without weapons. Most hunters use weapons that can kill things at a distance. Today we have guns, but long before guns were invented, hunters were using spears, slings, or bows and arrows.

STRING AND STONES

Unless you can throw stones very hard, they probably will not kill the animal. A sling is a long string with a pouch in the middle. You put a stone in the pouch and hold the two ends of the string to whirl the stone around your head. When you let go of one end of the string, the stone flies off much faster than you could throw it.

BOWS AND ARROWS

A bow is a long stick that is held in a curved shape by string that has been tied to its ends. When you use a bow to shoot an arrow, you pull back on the string. This bends the bow even more. Bending the bow stores energy in it. When you let go of the string and the arrow, all this energy is released at once and pushes the arrow forwards at great speed. The harder it is to pull your bow, the faster the arrow will travel when you let go.

An atlatl, or throwing stick, can be used to help you to throw a spear further. The atlatl effectively makes your arm longer. The further the end of the spear is from your shoulder when you swing your arm, the faster it will be moving and the further it will go.

see for yourself

You can buy throwing toys for dogs that are balls with a piece of rope or string attached. These are similar to throwing the ball using a sling. You can also buy throwers that have a cup for the ball on the end of a handle and these act like an atlatl. Find out how well these work by seeing how far you can throw a ball with and without a thrower.

The feathers on the back of an arrow help it to fly more accurately and hit the target.

HOW TO JOURNEY TO THE MIDDLE OF THE EARTH

Caves are holes in the ground that have been formed naturally. The deepest known cave in the world is more than 6,560 ft (2,000 m) from top to bottom, and it may go even deeper.

MINES

A mine is a place where coal, diamonds, or metals, such as gold, are taken out of the ground. Most mines are shafts and tunnels dug into the Earth. The deepest mine is a gold mine in South Africa that is nearly 2.5 miles (4 km) deep.

A mine is not a very comfortable place to be. The only light comes from lamps and it can be very hot. As you go deeper into the Earth, the temperature gets higher. Down deep mines, the temperature can get as high as 131°F (55°C)—this is too hot for humans to survive for long periods of time. You would also run out of oxygen quickly, as the wind cannot blow through the mine to bring fresh air to you. Mines need to have fans to blow air through them, and deep ones need air conditioning equipment to cool them down.

BOREHOLES

A borehole is a narrow hole drilled into the ground. Some boreholes are used to get water, and some are drilled to investigate the rocks beneath the Earth's surface. Pressure increases as you dig deeper, so it is very difficult to keep the hole from collapsing.

The world's deepest borehole is the Kola Superdeep Borehole in Russia. It is 7.5 miles (12 km) deep. This is less than half the distance through the top layer of the Earth.

SEISMIC WAVES AND METEORITES

Scientists have worked out what the inside of the Earth

LAYERS IN THE EARTH

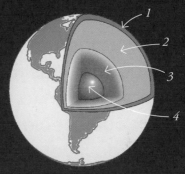

The Earth is not the same all the way through, but is made of layers.

1. We live on the crust
2. The mantle is solid rock
3. The outer core is liquid, and is mostly made of iron and nickel
4. The inner core is solid, and is also mostly iron and nickel

earthquakes. The planets and meteorites in the solar system formed from the same cloud of dust and gas, so scientists can work out the kinds of rock that are inside the Earth from the materials in meteorites.

Earthquakes send waves out through the Earth, a bit like ripples on water. Scientists can detect these seismic waves at different places around the world, and work out the way they have traveled

30 HOW TO SURVIVE A SNAKE BITE

The most venomous land snake is the inland taipan, which is found in Australia. One bite from this snake has enough venom to kill 100 people! There are more than 600 species of venomous snake, so what should you do if you get bitten by one?

VENOMOUS SNAKES

The poison that some snakes produce is called venom. Venom is dangerous only if it gets into your blood directly, so you can safely drink most kinds of snake venom! Only a fraction of all the snake species in the world are venomous. Almost every country in the world has some venomous snakes, but some countries have more than others.

Snakes do not hunt humans for food—we are too big for them! Snakes usually bite people only when they are startled or disturbed. You are more likely to step on or disturb a snake that is camouflaged (blends in with its surroundings) than one that is brightly colored. You are also more likely to come across a snake that is common than one that is rare. The snakes with the most deadly venom are not necessarily the most dangerous.

WHEN YOU ARE BITTEN

The effects of a snake bite depend on the kind of snake that bit you. A bite from a non-venomous snake can still be harmful because the wound could become

☞ *Many snake charmers avoid bites by removing the fangs from their snakes, or even sewing their mouths shut.*

VENOM AND FANGS

Snakes inject venom through their fangs (the big teeth in the front of their mouths). The venom is made in glands in their heads.

Venom is pushed along this tube

Venom gland

Venom shoots out through a hole in the end of each fang

Muscle to push out venom

the animal it bites. It injects venom only if it wants to kill the animal for food. A dry bite, like the bite from a non-venomous snake, can be dangerous if it gets infected.

The area around a snake bite usually becomes red and painful, and may swell up. You may feel weak, dizzy, and sick. Some kinds of venom can make your blood stop clotting, so your nose and mouth may bleed.

infected. A venomous snake does not always inject venom when it bites something. This is called a "dry bite." A snake giving a dry bite is warning off

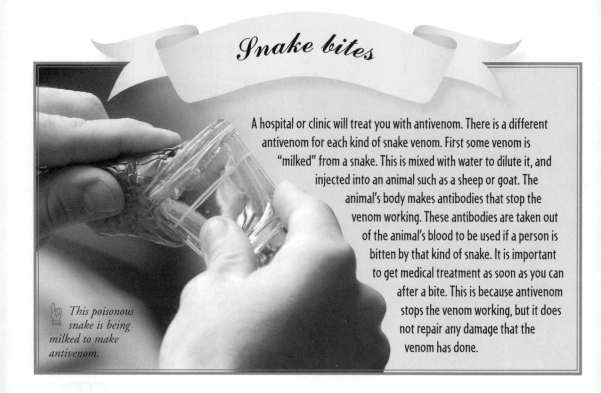

Snake bites

A hospital or clinic will treat you with antivenom. There is a different antivenom for each kind of snake venom. First some venom is "milked" from a snake. This is mixed with water to dilute it, and injected into an animal such as a sheep or goat. The animal's body makes antibodies that stop the venom working. These antibodies are taken out of the animal's blood to be used if a person is bitten by that kind of snake. It is important to get medical treatment as soon as you can after a bite. This is because antivenom stops the venom working, but it does not repair any damage that the venom has done.

This poisonous snake is being milked to make antivenom.

You may also bleed inside your body, which can be very dangerous. Some venom attacks your nerves, and you could stop breathing if you do not get medical treatment.

The good news is that if you live in a country with good hospitals and supplies of antivenom, most snake bites can be treated successfully. Even if the wound does not feel sore or look swollen, get medical help. Not all venomous bites cause problems immediately.

WHAT TO DO IF YOU ARE BITTEN

If you are bitten by a snake, the most important thing is to make sure you are not bitten again! Do not risk another bite by trying to kill or capture the snake.

Keep calm. If you panic or run around, your blood will move around your body faster and cause the venom to spread quicker. Call for help or get someone to drive you to the nearest hospital.

If you were bitten on the leg or arm, rest with the bitten part below the level of your heart and keep as still as possible. This will help to stop the venom spreading through your body. Your arm or leg may swell up, so take off any bracelets, rings, watches, or shoes. Do not eat or drink anything, including painkillers.

EATING PREY

Some snakes that do not have venom can still kill you! Snakes such as boa constrictors or pythons kill their prey by squeezing them. But all snakes have the same problem once they have killed their meal.

They cannot tear it up into smaller chunks, so they have to swallow it whole. Snakes can expand their jaws to swallow animals much wider than they are. Once they have swallowed its prey, snakes will rest until the animal has been digested. Large snakes, such as pythons, have been known to eat whole deer or sheep.

This young boa constrictor has dislocated its jaws to eat its lunch!

31 HOW TO SURVIVE IN SPACE

You survive on the Earth because you breathe the air, and have water to drink and food to eat. But it is not so easy in space—there is no air to breathe, no rain, and no food! You can live inside a spacesuit for a short time, but if you are going to be spending more than a few hours in space, you will need a spacecraft that supplies you with all the essentials.

AIR

Every time you breathe, your body takes some oxygen out of the air and adds carbon dioxide. Without oxygen you will die, and you will also die if there is too much carbon dioxide in the air. Astronauts need a supply of oxygen. This can be taken up to the space station in tanks of compressed gas. Oxygen can also be made from water using electricity from solar panels, but then the water needs to be taken up instead. A space station has special equipment that removes carbon dioxide from the air. Fans keep the air moving around the space station.

WATER

You must drink water to live and this water comes out of you again. You breathe out water vapor, you lose water when you sweat and when you go to the toilet. In a space station, all water is recycled, even urine from the toilets! It is purified before the astronauts drink it again.

ELECTRICITY

All the equipment used to provide breathable air, drinkable water, and a comfortable temperature in space needs electricity. For a short flight this can be provided by fuel cells, which combine hydrogen and oxygen to make water and electricity at the same time. The International Space Station uses solar panels to convert sunlight into electricity.

Solar panels

☞ *Astronauts may have to spend many hours on a spacewalk. How long do you think they would survive without a spacesuit?*

111

Astronauts on the Vomit Comet have to get used to being weightless before they go into space.

TEMPERATURE

Sunlight passes through the atmosphere before it warms the Earth (and us), but in space there is no air to absorb the heat. Spacecraft have insulation to stop heat going in and out of them. This insulation works so well that the main problem is how to keep cool! Computers, air purifiers, lights, and the astronauts' bodies all produce heat. There are coolers to keep the inside of the spacecraft at a comfortable temperature.

BEING WEIGHTLESS

Astronauts in a spacecraft are "weightless." They float around inside the spacecraft, and so does their food, drink, and anything else that is not tied down. If you have seen videos of astronauts in space, this looks like fun, but it also causes problems.

Astronauts have to drink liquid through straws. If a bit of liquid escapes, it floats around as a little ball. Liquid or crumbs from food can damage electrical equipment if they get inside the equipment.

The lack of gravity affects how the human body works. Astronauts often have stuffy noses and suffer from flatulence (they fart a lot!). But one of the most unpleasant parts of being weightless is "space sickness." About half of all astronauts suffer from travel sickness when they first go into space, and some of them vomit a lot.

THE VOMIT COMET

Astronauts can get used to the feeling of weightlessness before they go into space by riding on the "Vomit Comet." This is an

airplane without seats and with lots of padding inside. The airplane flies up and then down again—as it is coming down, the astronauts inside it feel weightless. The weightlessness lasts for about half a minute, and the airplane can fly the same pattern many times in one flight.

Exercise in space

Muscles do not have to work very hard in space, and they can get very weak. Bones do not have to support the body against the pull of gravity, and they get thinner and weaker in space. After only a few months in space an astronaut could be as weak as a very elderly person, and likely to break bones very easily. To prevent this, astronauts use special treadmills, with harnesses to hold them down. They have to exercise for at least two hours each day.

32 HOW TO TURN YOURSELF INTO A ROBOT

You may think of a robot as something that looks a bit like a human, with arms and legs, but robots can be almost any shape or size. A robot is a machine that can control itself.

WHAT CAN ROBOTS DO?

Some robots are very simple. For example, you can buy a robot to cut grass. All it does is cut grass, turning around when it reaches a wire that marks the edge of the lawn. Many factories use robots to build cars or other items. Even a washing machine is a kind of robot: it has a mini computer to control the washing, rinsing, and spin-drying. These robots do not look anything like the grass-cutting robot. And if you wanted to be a robot, you would probably want to be one that looked like a human!

EXOSKELETONS

An exoskeleton is a skeleton that is outside the body. Your skeleton inside your body helps to keep your body the right shape. Muscles can pull on the different bones in your skeleton to move your arms, legs, and fingers.

If you had a robot puppy, you could program it to take itself for a walk... and pick up its own poop!

A robot exoskeleton fits around your body, or part of your body, such as the legs. Motors in the exoskeleton can make the legs move in the same way as your own legs do. This can help you to lift heavier weights. More importantly, exoskeletons could be used for people whose own legs are too weak, or whose muscles do not work. People who use wheelchairs could use exoskeletons instead.

WHAT DO YOU NEED TO MAKE A ROBOT?

The robot dog opposite has a stiff body with joints so it can move around. It has motors inside it to move the joints. It has a battery to store energy to power the motors. It can hear what you say to it, and it can see things around it. It also has a computer to receive information from its "ears" and "eyes," and to tell the motors what to do. You can make yourself a bit like a robot, by replacing individual body parts. These might help you to run faster, be stronger, or to do things such as seeing in the dark.

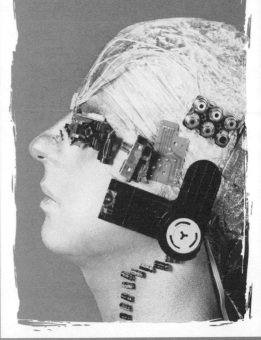

ARTIFICIAL LIMBS

People who have been in a car crash or other accident may lose a leg. They can have an artificial leg fitted so that they can still walk. The most basic artificial leg is just a peg, perhaps with a foot fitted. You can put a shoe on the foot so that when you are wearing trousers it is not obvious that you have an artificial leg.

But you can get much better legs than this. One modern artificial leg has a small computer and shock absorbers, and can let the person walk, run, and ride a bicycle just as if he or she still had a real leg. The only problem is that it costs about three times as much as a family car!

But even a simple artificial leg can allow you to be a runner. An athlete using two artificial legs was banned from the Olympic Games in 2008 because it was thought that the springy legs would give him an advantage over other athletes. However, scientists have studied runners with one of these legs and found that there is no advantage over people who still have both their legs.

This runner is able to run in races for disabled athletes. "Blade runners" have competed in races from sprints to the marathon.

Feedback

Can you pick up an egg without breaking it? Of course you can–but this is a very difficult task for a robot! You can do it without thinking but your body is automatically doing a lot of things!

Your eyes detect the egg, and your brain sends signals to your arm to move your hand to the egg. Your brain tells your hand to open and to put your fingers and thumb around the egg. Then your brain sends signals to your fingers to close. When you touch the egg, you can feel the pressure in your fingers. Your brain tells your hand to carry on squeezing tighter until the pressure is just right. When you were a baby you learned how much pressure in your fingers is needed to pick up different objects. When the pressure is right, your brain tells your fingers to keep that pressure while your arm moves up. If your fingers feel the egg slipping, your brain will tell

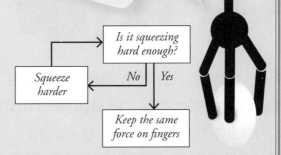

Is it squeezing hard enough?

Squeeze harder

No   Yes

Keep the same force on fingers

your fingers to squeeze a little harder. So a robot needs a camera to "see" the egg, and a computer program that can work out which part of the picture is the egg. It needs pressure sensors in its "fingers." The computer needs to be programmed with "feedback" so it can pick up the egg without squeezing too hard and breaking it.

This robot uses feedback systems that enable it to play table tennis.

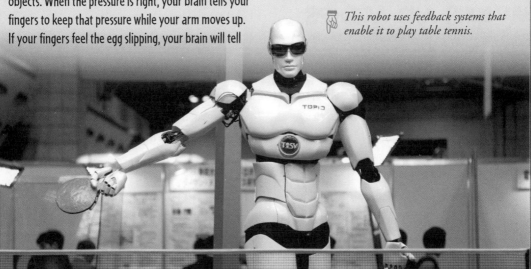

33 HOW TO MAKE A FLYING MACHINE

Birds, bats, and many insects can fly, but they are all quite small and light. How can a huge passenger jet full of people get into the air? And will we ever have our own personal flying machines?

BALLOONS AND AIRSHIPS

The first flying machines were hot-air balloons. These were huge "envelopes" made out of silk or other fabrics, with a fire built beneath them to fill them with hot air. Hot air is less dense than cold air, and makes the balloon float upwards. Later balloons were filled with hydrogen or helium. These are both gases that are less dense than air.

Balloons do not have an engine, so they can only go where the winds take them. An airship is a large balloon with engines and propellers to move it through the air. Today many people fly hot-air balloons for fun. There are also small airships filled with helium that take people on sightseeing trips.

GLIDERS

A glider has wings, but no engine. The first gliders looked like modern hang-gliders, but the pilot had to run down a hillside to get into the air. Today's gliders look more like planes. These gliders must be pulled into the air using a winch on the ground, or towed up behind an airplane. With no engine, gliders cannot go upwards without help from the wind. Glider pilots look for places where the wind is being forced upwards over hills or cliffs, or for thermals (rising columns of warm air over towns or other warm places). Using the wind or thermals, today's gliders can stay in the air for many hours, and can cover vast distances if the conditions are right.

He may have wings, but this jet-propelled daredevil doesn't fly very well. He still needs to jump out of a plane or a balloon.

see for yourself

Get a piece of stiff card, such as the back of a large notepad. Hold it horizontally and run, so that the air is moving over the card. Now tilt the card up a little at the front and run again. Can you feel the lift from the tilted card?

GETTING A LIFT

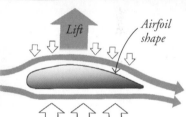

Lift

Airfoil shape

More air pushes up than down.

The force that keeps an airplane in the air is called lift. Most of the lift is provided by the plane's wings. The wings have an airfoil shape, which forces the air downwards underneath it. The pressure from the air underneath the wings is greater than the pressure from the air above them, and this difference in pressure pushes the wings upwards. The amount of lift depends on how big the wings are and how fast they are moving through the air. The bigger the wings and the faster the airplane is moving, the greater the lift.

POWERED FLIGHT

The first flight by an airplane with an engine was made by the Wright brothers in the USA in 1903. That airplane went just 118 ft (36 m) and carried only the pilot. Today, the biggest planes can carry 800 people 9,000 miles (15,000 km). These planes accelerate to 180 mph (290 km/h) before they can take off, and cruise at about 550 mph (885 km/h).

TAKE A FLIGHT

You are at the end of the runway, cleared for take-off. You put the flaps down— these are parts of the wing that move down and backwards to give more lift for take-off and landing. You increase the engine speed and let go of the brakes. The plane moves faster and faster, until you reach take-off speed. You pull the control column towards you. This moves the tail flaps that push the back of the plane down and tilt the front upwards, and you notice that the ground is getting further away. You reach cruising speed and put up the flaps. When it is time to land, you line up the plane with the runway and push in the throttle to slow down. You put the flaps down and descend gently to the tarmac. If you have got it right, there will be a gentle bump, and then you can put the brakes on.

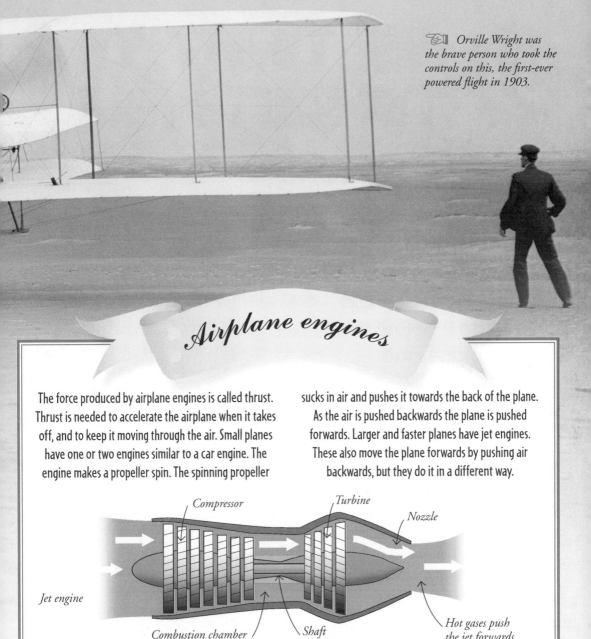

Airplane engines

The force produced by airplane engines is called thrust. Thrust is needed to accelerate the airplane when it takes off, and to keep it moving through the air. Small planes have one or two engines similar to a car engine. The engine makes a propeller spin. The spinning propeller sucks in air and pushes it towards the back of the plane. As the air is pushed backwards the plane is pushed forwards. Larger and faster planes have jet engines. These also move the plane forwards by pushing air backwards, but they do it in a different way.

Compressor

Turbine

Nozzle

Jet engine

Combustion chamber

Shaft

Hot gases push the jet forwards

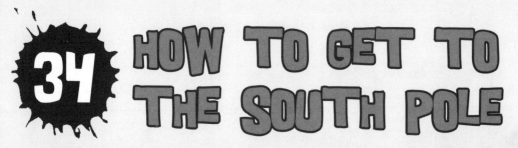

34 HOW TO GET TO THE SOUTH POLE

The South Pole is in the middle of the Antarctic. Scientists and other people wanting to get to one of the research stations in the Antarctic usually fly. But can you get there without an airplane? And how did people do it before there were airplanes that could fly in those conditions?

AMUNDSEN AND DOGS

The first expedition to reach the South Pole was led by Roald Amundsen, a Norwegian explorer. The expedition arrived there on December 14, 1911, which is in the middle of summer in the Antarctic.

Amundsen's party arrived in the Antarctic in January 1911. They spent months traveling south to leave supplies along the way. Setting out in the spring, dogs were used to pull sleds with the expedition's food and tents, while the men skied. The dogs were from Greenland and had been bred as sled dogs. Once they were nearly at the pole, half the dogs were killed and used as food for the other dogs. This meant that they did not have to pull as much weight.

RACE TO THE POLE

At the same time, a British expedition led by Captain Robert Scott was also trying to get to the South Pole. This became a race to see which country could get its people there first. Scott's party did not reach the South Pole until January 17, 1912.

Scott had used motor vehicles for part of the way, but they broke down. They had also used ponies, which they killed and ate when the ponies could not go any further. They finally pulled their sleds themselves. Unfortunately, this made the men so weak that they all died on the way back to their ship.

WHAT TO WEAR

It is very cold in the Antarctic, even in summer. Your clothes must keep you warm, but if you are skiing or working you may get hot. Your clothes also need to be designed to deal with sweat and keep you comfortable. This can be done by wearing lots of layers.

"Wicking" underwear to carry sweat away from your body

Fleecy layers to help keep in your body heat

Clothes filled with down (tiny feathers) trap the heat and are really warm

Thick gloves, boots, and a hat keep your hands, feet, and head warm, and goggles protect your eyes

The Earth is a sphere and it spins–this is what gives us day and night. The Earth's axis is tilted (compared to its orbit around the Sun), and this gives us seasons. When it is summer in the northern hemisphere it is winter in the southern hemisphere. It is summer in the Antarctic at the same time of year that it is summer in countries such as Australia, New Zealand, South America, and the southern parts of Africa.

Winter in the Arctic

Sun

Dark for six months at the North Pole

South Pole tilted towards the Sun

Summer in the Antarctic

North Pole tilted towards the Sun

Summer in the Arctic

Dark for six months at the South Pole

Sun

Winter in the Antarctic

SUN PROTECTION

Sunlight includes a kind of light called ultraviolet (UV). We cannot see ultraviolet light, but it is this part of sunlight that gives us sunburn. It can also damage our eyes, so you need sunglasses or goggles to cut out the ultraviolet. You also need to wear plenty of sunscreen.

It is important to be protected against ultraviolet light in Antarctica. Ozone gas in the atmosphere blocks most of the ultraviolet light from the Sun and stops it reaching the Earth's surface. However, there is less ozone over Antarctica than over other places in the world, so there is more ultraviolet light. Also, ultraviolet light is absorbed by the ground in most other places in the world, but the snow and ice

in the Antarctic reflect it. This means you can even get sunburned under your chin or inside your nose if you are not careful!

GETTING THERE TODAY

Scientists go to Antarctica to investigate the weather or the atmosphere. The long night is also very good for astronomers, because there is no pollution to spoil the view of the stars. All these scientists need to get to their bases and back, and they need food, fuel, and other supplies.

Most of the transport is by airplane. The planes usually have skis fitted around their wheels so they do not sink in snow. There is also a road from the harbor at McMurdo Station to the South Pole. Vehicles with tracks (like bulldozers) can travel on it.

People still like to get to the South Pole without airplanes or trucks. Many walk to the South Pole as a challenge, or to raise money for charity. You will need to tow a sled behind you with your food and tent in it. Even if you are very fit, getting to the South Pole will take you at least a month.

Getting to the South Pole on foot is much easier than it was for Scott. Modern materials mean that warm clothes are very effective and sleds can be light. Maps and satellite photographs can help you to plan the route, and we know much more about food and nutrition. Scott's party may have died partly because they became very unhealthy through not having the right types of food with them.

HOW TO SURVIVE ON A DESERT ISLAND

Could you survive if you were shipwrecked or your plane crashed and you ended up on a desert island? There would be no one there to help you. What would you need to do to survive?

SURVIVING

If your desert island is very hot, you will survive for just a couple of days unless you can keep cool and have water to drink. You can live longer without food, but you will be very hungry! So the first things you need to do on your island are to find somewhere to keep out of the Sun, and find some fresh water to drink. Anything you can collect from the shipwreck could be useful as well.

WATER

If you are lucky, your desert island will have a stream from which you can drink. If not, you will have to make fresh water from seawater.

You must not drink seawater, because it has a lot of salt in it and will make you very ill.

see for yourself

Stir some salt into a glass of water, until no more salt will dissolve. Then pour some of the salty water into a saucer and put this on a warm, sunny windowsill. After a few days you will see that the pure water has evaporated, leaving behind the salt in the saucer.

You can make fresh water from seawater by distillation—but only if you can find some plastic and some containers to hold the water!

DISTILLING AND FILTERING

If you take water from the sea you need to filter it first to get rid of any sand or small sea creatures. You can do this by pouring it through a piece of cloth. The cloth traps the sand particles and lets the water run through. Filtering cannot get the salt out of seawater because the salt is dissolved in the water. This means that the salt has broken up into minute particles. These are almost the same size as the particles that make up water, and they will go through anything that the water will go through.

You can separate the salt and water by distillation, using a solar still. The solar still works because heat from the Sun makes the water, but not the salt, evaporate. The water vapor condenses when it reaches the plastic sheet. The drips run down the sheet and into the empty container.

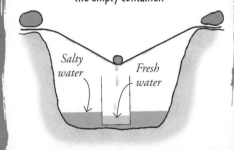

Salty water

Fresh water

SUNBURN AND HEATSTROKE

If you stay out in the Sun too long, your skin will become sunburned. This may just make your skin go red and feel hot, but if you get badly sunburned you may get blisters on your skin, and it may start to peel off. The best way to prevent sunburn is to stay out of the Sun, or to wear clothes and a hat that cover your skin and shade your face.

Staying out of the Sun as much as you can will also help to avoid heatstroke. Your body keeps itself at the right temperature by shivering if you are too cold and sweating if you are too hot. (You can find out how sweating works on page 159.) Sometimes your body gets warmer faster than sweating can cool it down again. If you do not drink enough water, your body will not be able to keep sweating and your body temperature will rise. You might feel sick and dizzy and

☞ You need a shelter to protect you from the Sun. It needs to let the air through, to help keep you cool.

have a headache. If you get too hot, you could even die! So it is important to stay out of the Sun as much as you can.

Make a shelter to keep the Sun off you, but build it so that breezes can blow through to keep you cool.

Making a fire

Once you have a shelter and have made some drinking water, you will probably be hungry! You may be able to find some berries or other fruit to eat, but you may have to trap or catch some animals for food. (You can read more about hunting on page 102.) These will taste much nicer if you can cook them—for this you will need a fire. You could also use a fire to make smoke that passing ships or airplanes might see.

One way of making fire is by friction. You may have heard of "rubbing sticks together" to make a fire. Rubbing two things together makes them warmer. The drawing below shows one way of rubbing together pieces of wood fast enough to make a fire.

If you wear glasses you might be lucky and have an easier way of making a fire. If you are long-sighted (you can see distant things clearly without your glasses, but not close things), your glasses will act as magnifying lenses. Hold your glasses so that the light from the Sun is focused into a small, bright patch. Aim the patch at some dry leaves or grass, and they will eventually get hot enough to make a fire.

String looped around stick

Bow made from string and bendy stick

Pointed stick

Hole in piece of dry wood

36 HOW TO GROW A NEW BODY

If you cut yourself or graze your knee, after a few days the damaged skin grows back. But if you have a really bad accident and lose a leg or an arm, you cannot grow a new one. Will we ever be able to grow ourselves new bodies?

ORGANS AND TRANSPLANTS

Some people's kidneys, heart, or lungs may not work properly. Our bodies cannot grow whole new organs, but these people may be able to get new organs by having a transplant.

If a healthy person dies suddenly, for example in an accident, relatives may allow some of his or her organs to be used to help a sick person. For example, the dead person's heart can be put into someone whose heart is failing.

The patient who receives the heart will need to be given drugs for the rest of his or her life to stop the body rejecting the new heart. This can happen because our bodies have ways of protecting us against diseases. The patient's body recognizes the new heart as something that does not "belong" to it, and tries to reject it.

All your organs were new before you were born. This ultrasound image shows a fetus in its mother's womb.

CELLS AND ORGANS

You started life as an egg inside your mother. The egg was just one cell. When the egg started to grow into you, this cell split to form a ball of cells, called an embryo. So far, all the cells were the same as each other. But then as the cells kept on dividing, they began to turn into different kinds of cells.

Cells are the smallest parts of your body. Cells work together in organs, with each organ having a particular job. Your heart is made from muscle and nerve cells, and pumps blood around your body. Other organs include your brain, stomach, skin, liver, and kidneys.

Some cells have tiny strands on the top to move things past them. Your windpipe is lined with cells like this

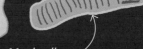

Muscle cells can change length

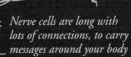

Nerve cells are long with lots of connections, to carry messages around your body

ORGAN DONATION

There are never enough organs for donation. This is a good thing in some ways, as organs become available only when someone dies. But it means that some patients will die while they are waiting for a transplant. It may soon be possible to use organs from animals, such as pigs, instead of having to wait for a suitable human donor.

A baby starts to grow when an egg cell inside a woman is fertilized by sperm from a man. Some couples cannot have babies naturally, and may use "in vitro fertilization," or IVF. In IVF, eggs are removed from a woman and the sperm is added in a dish in a laboratory. Usually several eggs from the woman are fertilized at once. When the fertilized eggs begin to divide, one or two of the healthiest embryos are put back into the woman to grow into babies. The spare embryos may be frozen, in case the couple want another baby later. But many of these embryos are never used.

The cells in the embryos are "stem cells." They have not started to become specialized. Most of the stem cells used to find out how to grow new organs come from unused embryos. Some people think that this is wrong, because this kills the embryo. Other people say this does not matter, because the embryo was not going to be used to make a baby.

☞ *In the future, scientists may be able to grow new arms or legs for humans, just like salamanders grow new tails.*

SALAMANDERS AND LOSING LEGS

If people lose arms or legs in accidents, they cannot grow new limbs (although they can be given artificial limbs—you can read more about this on page 116). But some animals, such as newts, salamanders, and geckos, can grow new limbs. This is because when they get injured, cells near the injury turn back into the kind of cells in an embryo.

GROWING NEW ORGANS

Scientists can treat some patients using stem cells from embryos. So far they have not managed to make complete organs, such as a new heart or liver. But they can inject stem cells into certain organs that are not working properly to make them work better.

GROWING A NEW BODY

It will probably be possible, some time in the future, to grow an entire new body. But what about your brain? The memories and all the other things that make you "you" are in your brain. If a new brain was put into your body, would you still be "you"? Or would you be just a body with no memories and no personality? So it may never be possible to have a completely new body!

37 HOW TO MAKE AN EXPLOSION

This photograph shows an explosion being used to demolish a building. Explosives are also useful in quarrying stone. But explosions can sometimes happen accidentally and cause a lot of damage.

EXPLOSIONS

An explosion happens when a lot of energy is suddenly released. Explosions caused by humans are usually chemical reactions that happen very fast and release a lot of gas. The gas is hot and expands suddenly. This sudden expansion makes the bang that you hear. Explosions are more common than you may think—in car engines, a mix of fuel and air explodes thousands of times each second!

People make small explosions when they open champagne. Bottles of champagne have a cork in the top, held on with wire. If you take off the wire and shake the bottle, you can fire the cork a long way! This happens because champagne has carbon dioxide gas dissolved in it. When you shake the bottle, the gas goes into the air space above the liquid, and the pressure builds up. When the pressure is high enough it pushes the cork out of the bottle.

ACCIDENTAL EXPLOSIONS

The gasoline used in car engines evaporates easily, and burns quickly if it is mixed with air. A smoldering cigarette end could light a mixture of fuel and air and cause an explosion. This is why smoking is banned in gas stations.

Even ordinary things such as flour or sawdust can explode if the conditions are right. These explosions happen when the flour or sawdust is in the air as a dust. If part of it catches fire, the flame then spreads quickly through the dust and causes an explosion.

ALFRED NOBEL

The Nobel prizes are awarded each year for important discoveries in science, for literature, and for helping the world to become more peaceful. The prizes were set up when Alfred Nobel died and left a lot of money in his will. Nobel made most of his money from selling explosives and guns. He invented dynamite and gelignite. These were powerful explosives, but they were also safe to use. In other words, they only exploded when you wanted them to! Some earlier explosives were very dangerous, because they could explode without warning.

Guns and bullets

The first guns were quite difficult to use. You first had to put gunpowder into the gun, taking care not to get it wet. Then you had to put in the bullet, and use a "ramrod" to push the bullet and the powder all the way to the end of the gun barrel. Then you put some more powder in a little pan on the top of the gun and fastened a piece of "slow match" next to it. A slow match is a length of thin rope that burns very slowly. When it was time to fire the gun, the trigger moved the slow match into the powder in the pan and set it alight.

Barrel

Gunpowder and bullet inside here

Pan

Slow match

This made the gunpowder inside the gun explode. The expanding gases from the explosion fired the bullet out of the front of the gun. Modern guns are much quicker to load. The gun opens so the bullets can be put into the back of the gun instead of having to be pushed all the way along the barrel. The explosive is part of the bullet itself, so you do not need to worry about keeping your powder dry!

FIREWORKS

Fireworks use an explosive called black powder. A big firework that bursts in the air has two separate charges of black powder. The first charge is used to shoot the firework up into the air. Then, a separate "bursting charge" explodes, and shoots the "stars" outwards in all directions. The stars are made of similar materials to sparklers. They do not explode, but burn slowly for several seconds. The "sparks" are made by tiny bits of metal in the mixture burning.

The different colors in fireworks are made by adding different metals to the mixture. Red colors are made using chemicals containing strontium or lithium, yellow is made using sodium, and blue can be made using copper. Aluminum or magnesium give silvery colors.

NATURAL EXPLOSIONS

Explosions can occur naturally. Volcanoes sometimes throw out runny lava, but sometimes the lava gets trapped inside them. The pressure builds up until the volcano explodes. (You can read more about volcanoes on pages 40–43). Meteorites can also cause explosions. Most meteors burn up as they fall through the atmosphere, but if a big one hits the ground it may cause an explosion. (You can read more about meteorites on pages 52–53.)

Even stars can explode! Our Sun sometimes has explosions on its surface. These cause "solar flares" that may interfere with satellites and can even damage the wires that send electricity around the country. And stars that are bigger than the Sun will explode at the end of their life.

see for yourself

You can make your own explosion using Mentos mints and diet cola. Drop a couple of the mints into a bottle of the drink and stand back! The mints react with the drink creating huge amounts of foam, which explodes out of the bottle.

38 HOW TO MAKE A RAINBOW

How is this photograph of a cat peering through a fish bowl connected to rainbows? The bowl of water is acting as a lens, because the direction of light changes as it travels through the bowl. This effect is called refraction. Refraction can also make rainbows.

MAKING RAINBOWS

The light we normally see does not seem to have a color. Scientists call it white light. But white light is made up of a mixture of different colors. When we see all the colors at once, our brains interpret this as white light. When sunlight shines through raindrops, the light is split into the separate colors, and we see a rainbow.

MIRAGES

Have you ever been walking along a straight road on a hot, sunny day, and noticed that the ground ahead looks as if it has water on it? You are seeing a

mirage. Mirages occur because of refraction. The air near the ground is heated by the hot ground, and it has a different density to the air higher up. The change in density makes light going through the air bend. What you are seeing in a mirage is actually a kind of reflection of the sky!

see for yourself

You can see a spectrum using a CD. Look at the side with no label, and angle it towards a light. You should see mini rainbows in it. The CD has lots of tiny grooves running around it, which each reflect light. The rainbows on CDs are formed in a different way to the rainbows formed by water drops.

☞ *Refraction makes this cat's face look distorted when you see it through the fish bowl.*

HOW PRISMS AND RAINDROPS WORK

The colors in white light can be split up using a prism. Each color bends (refracts) by a slightly different amount as the light goes into the prism and comes out again. This makes the colors spread out to form a spectrum. A similar thing happens when light shines through drops of rain, but in this case the light is also reflected inside the drops. This is why you only see rainbows when you have the Sun behind you.

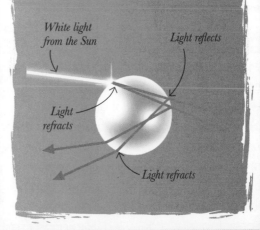

White light from the Sun

Light reflects

Light refracts

Light refracts

39 HOW TO SPOT A FAKE

A fake is a copy of something that is passed off as the real thing. Ever since money was first used, people have been trying to copy it as an easy way of getting rich. But money is not the only thing that is faked. Other forgeries include works of art and passports that criminals and terrorists use to get in and out of countries.

COPYING MONEY

It used to be difficult to copy banknotes. The forger had to make an engraved "plate" to print counterfeit banknotes. Today, photocopiers and color printers make it easy to copy the patterns on a banknote. Making forged money is a crime everywhere, and in some countries the punishment used to be death! Spending fake money leads to price rises and people losing money when the faked bills are confiscated by the police.

The banks that print banknotes for their government include lots of security features. The bills are usually printed on good quality paper made of cotton or linen, which feels fairly stiff. They use a special printing process that leaves the lines of ink raised above the surface of the paper, so you can feel the ink. The patterns on the bills are also very complicated—if you look carefully you can see that parts of the pattern on a banknote are made up of tiny letters or numbers.

PAPER MONEY

Most banknotes are printed on paper with a watermark in it. If you hold the bill up to the light you can see a paler pattern or picture.

You can see the same pattern from both sides of the bill, because it is woven into the paper, not printed on it.

Some banknotes are printed on paper that has tiny colored threads woven into it, or a strip of metal foil. Some have holograms printed on them—these show different patterns if you hold them at different angles. And some are printed using special inks that change color depending on the angle at which you look at them, or only show up under ultraviolet (UV) light.

All these things make it harder for criminals to make copies of the bills. There are also some other security features, but the banks keep these secret so that criminals do not know what to copy. The banks can use these extra features to check batches of bills that they think might be fakes.

see for yourself

Look carefully at a banknote using a magnifying glass. Can you spot any of the features mentioned?

WORKS OF ART

Some paintings by famous artists can sell for more than $100 million. Someone who could make a good forgery could make a lot of money! There are ways of spotting fakes. If the forgery is pretending to be by an artist who lived a long time ago, scientists can find out how old the canvas is. If the canvas is not as old as the painting should be, then it is a fake!

Artists in the past used paints made from natural materials, such as colored earth, berries, or plants. Many modern paints are made in chemical factories. Tiny samples of the paint can be taken and tested. If the "old" painting was made using modern paints, then it is a fake.

When is a copy a crime?

Many people have a printed copy of a famous painting on their walls. Some people will pay a lot of money for a good painted copy of a painting by a famous artist. There is nothing wrong in making copies of paintings like this as long as you do not pretend that the painting was done by the original artist. And if the original artist is still alive, he or she has "copyright" in the painting and needs to give permission for the copying to be done.

Many artists also have a particular way of using their brush or applying the paint, and an expert can tell whether or not the painting is done in the correct style.

FAKE HOMEWORK

It is very easy to fake your homework. Lots of information is available on the Internet, and there are even websites that will let you buy essays to hand in as your own work. You may think this does not matter too much for a piece of homework, but it is still cheating. It matters even more if the faked work is being used to decide if you get a qualification at school, or if it is a piece of work at college that will help you to get a degree. Passing off copied ideas as your own is called plagiarism.

Most teachers can tell if you have copied your work from a website. Everyone has a writing style, and the style of the person who wrote the text is not likely to be the same as yours. Your teacher might also be suspicious if the work is too good! Many universities use software that compares your work with information available on the Internet, and detects when something has been copied.

☞ *This painting by Vincent van Gogh is just one of many famous paintings that fraudsters have tried to copy.*

40 HOW TO SAVE THE PLANET

The actions of human beings can affect the planet and the organisms living on it. Humans need a lot of resources, and in getting these we may pollute the air, sea, and land. What can we do to reduce the effect we are having on the Earth?

ONE PLANET

The Earth is the only planet we have. Some of the things that humans are doing will not destroy the Earth, but they will make it much more difficult for humans to live comfortably and safely here.

Once we have changed the Earth, we may not be able to fix it.

EXTINCTIONS

There are millions of different types of living things on the Earth. Scientists have identified and given scientific names to about 1.9 million different species of animals, plants, and other organisms. Humans (*Homo sapiens*) are just one of these species. Some scientists think that there are millions more species that have not yet been discovered. Most of these are probably microbes. Many of them may become extinct before we discover them.

A species becomes extinct when there are no more members of that species still alive. This can happen for many reasons. Sometimes a new disease might kill all the members of a species. The climate on the Earth has changed naturally many times in the past, and it may become too hot or too cold for a particular kind of animal or plant to survive. Or a new animal might move into the area and eat all of the prey animals or plants of one species.

MASS EXTINCTIONS

Sometimes many species become extinct within a few million years. (This is a very short time when you are talking about the history of the Earth!) There have been five "mass extinctions" that scientists know about. The last one was when the dinosaurs died out about 65 million years ago. This could have been due to a meteorite 6 miles (10 km) in diameter that hit the Earth at that time.

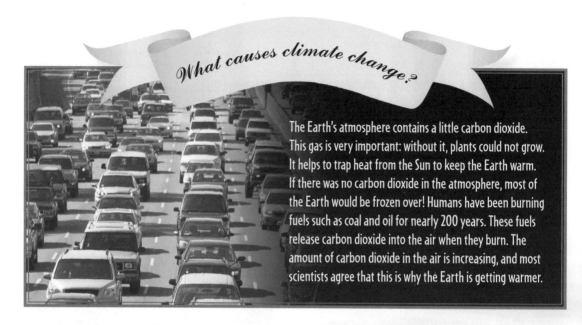

What causes climate change?

The Earth's atmosphere contains a little carbon dioxide. This gas is very important: without it, plants could not grow. It helps to trap heat from the Sun to keep the Earth warm. If there was no carbon dioxide in the atmosphere, most of the Earth would be frozen over! Humans have been burning fuels such as coal and oil for nearly 200 years. These fuels release carbon dioxide into the air when they burn. The amount of carbon dioxide in the air is increasing, and most scientists agree that this is why the Earth is getting warmer.

HUMANS AND EXTINCTIONS

The first five mass extinction events had natural causes. Many scientists think that we are now in the middle of a sixth mass extinction—caused by humans.

One famous extinct creature is the dodo. Dodos lived on an island in the Indian Ocean where there were no people. When ships started to call at the island, the dodos were not afraid of people because they had never seen them before. This made them very easy to kill for food and sport. Within 175 years, the dodo was extinct. Many other species have been made extinct by hunting. Humans can also make species extinct by destroying their habitats (the places where they live). We cut down forests to make the land available for farming, and build towns and cities on open land.

Habitats can also be destroyed by pollution (waste materials allowed to escape into the air or water). Many plants and animals that live in polluted areas may become extinct.

CLIMATE CHANGE

The world is gradually getting warmer. If you live somewhere very cold, you might think that this is a good thing, but it is not quite so simple! First of all, a warmer world means that ice in the Arctic and Antarctic will melt. Some of this will make sea levels rise. Some countries are very low and flat, and may flood if the seas rise.

Many animals and plants are adapted to live at a certain range of temperatures. If the world gets warmer, some animals may migrate to live in cooler areas, but the animals that already live in the coldest places will have nowhere to go. Most plants cannot suddenly change where they live.

A warmer world may also have different weather patterns. There may be more storms, or some places that used to get plenty of rain may become dry. All these changes could affect the way food crops grow, and so climate change may result in more people not having enough food to eat (you can read more about growing crops on pages 90–93).

SO WHAT CAN WE DO?

People all over the world need to work together to stop destroying habitats. We cannot stop the world getting warmer, but we might be able to stop the temperature going up too much if we put less carbon dioxide into the atmosphere. This means using wind or solar power to make electricity, and using cars less.

Polar bears live on pack ice in the Arctic. If the ice sheets melt, the bears could become extinct.

HOW TO FLY INTO SPACE

41

The first person went into space in 1961, and since then, more than 500 people have flown beyond Earth's atmosphere. Some have even walked on the Moon. But how did they get from the surface of the Earth into space?

BEYOND THE EARTH

Gravity is a force that tries to pull everything down. It is what is keeping you sitting in your chair instead of floating around. If you want to get into space you need to produce a force that will lift you up against the pull of gravity. Airplanes fly because the air moving over their wings produces a force called lift (see page 119). But there is no air in space, so wings, propellers, and jet engines would be useless.

☞ *Your own personal rocket pack might be fun, but it wouldn't get you into space!*

MOVING IN SPACE

When a rocket has gone into orbit around the Earth it does not need the engines any more—it will keep moving until another force acts on it, such as a blast from a rocket or the gravity of another planet. An airplane needs its engines all the time because the air it is moving through produces a force that tries to slow it down. This force is called friction (see page 12). There is no air in space, so there is no friction and the rocket keeps moving without having to use its engines.

ROCKET ENGINES

Almost all engines work by burning fuel, and fuels need oxygen to burn. As there is no air in space, spacecraft need to carry oxygen with them as well as fuel. The fuel and oxygen burn in the combustion chamber. The expanding gases push on the combustion chamber and the nozzle and provide the thrust that makes the rocket move.

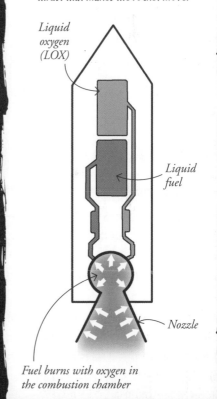

Liquid oxygen (LOX)

Liquid fuel

Nozzle

Fuel burns with oxygen in the combustion chamber

CARRYING WEIGHT

There are huge forces on a rocket, so it has to be very strong. This means it is heavy. It also has to carry all the fuel and oxygen needed to get it into space as well as the cargo or astronauts. The more weight it has to lift, the bigger the rocket needs to be and the more fuel and oxygen it will need to get into space. This makes it even heavier!

STAGES

This problem can be solved by throwing away parts (or stages) of the rocket when they have been used. For example, an Ariane 5 rocket has solid rocket boosters when it launches. These are dropped when their fuel runs out. The main stage is powered by liquid oxygen and liquid hydrogen. This stage, including the engine, is also dropped when the fuel is used up. The final stage has its own engine, fuel, and oxygen. It is only this part that carries on into orbit to launch a satellite.

REUSABLE SPACECRAFT

Using rockets with stages works, but you need a completely new rocket each time you want to send something into space. The space shuttle was designed to be reusable, although it still had bits that were thrown away during each launch! The astronauts and the satellites they took into space traveled in the orbiter. The rocket boosters were dropped when their fuel was used up, and parachuted down into the sea.

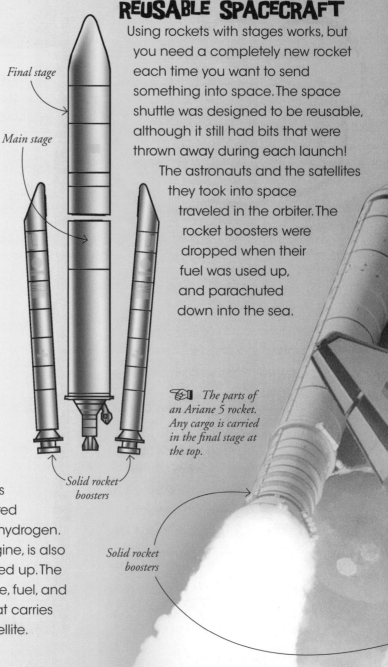

Final stage

Main stage

Solid rocket boosters

The parts of an Ariane 5 rocket. Any cargo is carried in the final stage at the top.

Solid rocket boosters

A boat collected them and sent them back to the factory to be checked and have more fuel put in. The external fuel tank did not have an engine. It carried liquid oxygen and hydrogen for the main engines in the orbiter. It was dropped when the space shuttle was 70 miles

External fuel tank (110 km) high, and broke up as it fell back to Earth. The orbiter did not need its wings when it took off, but it needed them when it came back to Earth. When it was coming in to land, the orbiter was the world's biggest and heaviest glider!

Orbiter

🚀 *Even with five powerful rockets, the space shuttle wasn't fast enough to fly out of Earth's orbit.*

So far, almost all the people who have been into space are astronauts employed by governments. There have been a few very rich people who have paid to have a flight to the International Space Station. Now there are private companies developing rockets that will take tourists into space.

SpaceShipTwo is one of these rockets. It will carry six passengers and two pilots on a flight lasting 2.5 hours, only a few minutes of which will be in space.

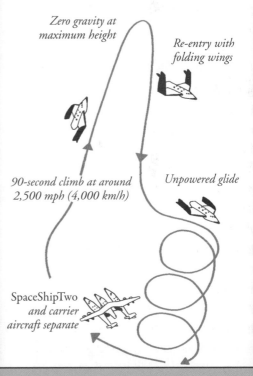

Zero gravity at maximum height

Re-entry with folding wings

90-second climb at around 2,500 mph (4,000 km/h)

Unpowered glide

SpaceShipTwo and carrier aircraft separate

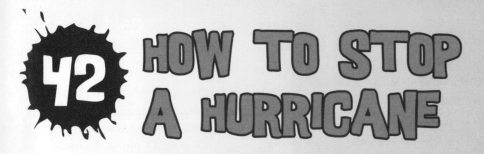

42 HOW TO STOP A HURRICANE

Hurricanes are storms with winds strong enough to demolish buildings. They bring torrential rain and can cause waves at sea up to 100 ft (30 m) high. The deadliest hurricane on record hit Texas in 1900, killing 8,000 people. Can hurricanes be stopped?

WHY HURRICANES HAPPEN

Hurricanes form over warm seas near the equator. Water evaporates from the warm sea, and the air above the sea is also warm. This warm, wet air rises and starts to spin. As it rises, it cools a little. Some of the water vapor in the air condenses and forms clouds that spread out around the center. When gases condense to form liquids, some heat is released. This heat warms the air in the center of the spinning column, and makes it rise even faster.

The rising air sucks in more warm, moist air from lower down. As long as the hurricane is over warm seas, it continues to blow and rotate, and may get bigger.

STOPPING A HURRICANE

A hurricane keeps going because it has a supply of warm, wet air from the sea. Hurricanes die out quickly once they cross from sea to land, but this does not help the people who suffer the wind, rain, and flooding. One idea for stopping a hurricane was to spread oil over the water where the hurricane would travel. This would stop water evaporating, and so the hurricane would get weaker and might even stop. However, the winds in hurricanes make rough waves and they broke up the oil layer. Other ideas have been to cool the air in the hurricane by using airplanes to drop chemicals onto it. One experiment showed that this reduced the wind speeds, but the wind increased again as soon as the airplane left. So far, no one has ever stopped a hurricane.

WHAT'S IN A NAME?

The scientific name for a hurricane is a "tropical cyclone." The term hurricane is used in Europe and the Americas. People in Asia call these storms "typhoons"–but a typhoon and a hurricane are the same thing.

Each hurricane or tropical storm is given a name. This makes it easier for scientists to talk about them if there is more than one at the same time. It also makes it easier for journalists to write about them in the news! If there is a very bad storm, such as Hurricane Katrina that hit the USA in 2005, that name is retired. The name Katrina will not be used again for a hurricane.

see for yourself

Make a model of a hurricane using two empty bottles. Fill one bottle three-quarters full with water. Turn the other one upside down and stick the necks of the bottles together with strong tape. Turn them upside down and give them a swirl. You will see a kind of hurricane as the water runs from the top bottle to the bottom.

43 HOW TO MAKE A FORCE FIELD

A force field is a place where there is a force on things even when nothing is touching them. Gravity makes a force field around the Earth that pulls everything towards the Earth. But there are other kinds of force fields that you can make yourself.

STATIC ELECTRICITY

The girl in the photograph is touching a machine that makes static electricity. Static electricity is what causes lightning, but it also makes a force field. Something that is charged with static electricity can attract other things towards it without having to touch them.

MAGNETISM

A magnet can pick up things made of certain metals: iron, steel, nickel, and cobalt. A magnet can attract these metals towards it without touching them. The area around the magnet where it has this effect is called its magnetic field.

Magnets can only attract pieces of metal, but if you have two magnets they can attract or repel (push) each other—all without having to touch.

The two ends of a magnet are called the north pole and the south pole (see Magnetic Earth on the next page to learn more about this). If you hold two magnets so that their north poles are close together you can feel them pushing apart. The same thing happens if you hold them with both south poles together. They attract each other only if you hold a north pole next to a south pole.

155

HOMING PIGEONS

Many people race homing pigeons as a hobby. All the pigeons in the race are put into baskets and taken many miles away. They are all released together and they fly back to their own loft. The journey is timed, and the pigeon that flies home the fastest wins the race.

Scientists are not quite sure exactly how pigeons find their way back home from hundreds of miles away. They think that it may involve detecting the Earth's magnetic field, using the angle of the Sun, or following smells.

Many birds migrate during the year to avoid cold weather when they would be short of food.

The bird with the longest migration is the Arctic tern. This bird breeds in the Arctic summer but flies right down to the Antarctic when it is summer there. It may fly more than 43,500 miles (70,000 km) in a single year!

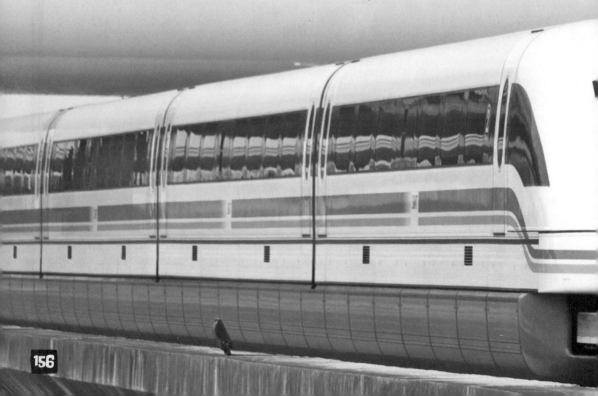

This train has no wheels! Electromagnets in the train and the track make it float above the track and move it forwards.

ELECTRICITY AND MAGNETS

Bar magnets and fridge magnets are permanent magnets. They are always magnetic. But sometimes you may want to be able to turn the magnetic field on and off, and for this you need electricity. An electromagnet is made using a coil of insulated wire. The electromagnet usually has a core made from iron. When an electric current flows through the coil, it has a magnetic field similar to the one around a bar magnet. When the current stops flowing, the magnetic field disappears.

The Earth has a magnetic field. If you tie a piece of thread around a bar magnet and let it hang down, it will turn so that one end points north. It is being attracted to the Magnetic North Pole of the Earth. This end of the magnet is called the "north-seeking pole." We usually shorten the name and call it the "north pole" of the magnet. The Earth's magnetic field is very useful for helping ships, airplanes, and hikers to find their way. Today, many people use satellite navigation (satnav) systems, but these are quite new. Before they were invented, people used a map and a compass to find their way. A compass has a small needle inside it that can swing around. The needle is magnetized so that it always points north. Once you know where north is, you can work out which way to turn your map to find your way.

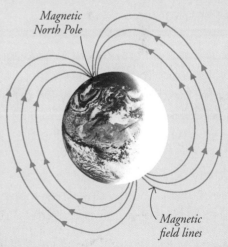

Magnetic North Pole

Magnetic field lines

44 HOW TO STAY COOL

Having a nice, cold drink on a hot day feels good. But how do we make things cold and stop them warming up again?

HUMIDITY AND STICKY DAYS

Have you ever been very sweaty on a warm day, without being able to cool down? Days like this are sometimes called "sticky" days, because of the way people feel when their sweat does not evaporate.

The air can hold only a certain amount of water vapor. The amount of water vapor in the air is the humidity. On a humid day (a day with high humidity) there is a lot of water vapor in the air.

On a dry day your sweat evaporates easily. But on a humid day, when there is already a lot of water vapor in the air, sweat does not evaporate as quickly. If it is very humid your sweat may not evaporate at all!

KEEPING THINGS COOL

If you want something cool to stay that way, you need to insulate it. Many people think of insulation as something that helps to keep things warm, but insulation can also keep things cool. This is because it stops heat being transferred from one thing to another.

Most insulation materials are fluffy, with lots of trapped air inside them. This is because air is a good insulator. Things can also be insulated by covering them in silvery material, because heat does not pass through shiny materials easily.

SWEATING

Your body needs to be kept at the correct temperature to work properly. If you are too hot, your skin produces sweat. The liquid sweat evaporates (turns into a gas), and as it does this it cools down. Evaporation happens faster if there is a breeze, because the breeze blows the evaporated water away.

Some animals keep cool in other ways. Dogs sweat only through their feet, so this does not really help them to keep cool. When a dog is trying to cool down, it pants. Panting moves air over its wet tongue, which cools it down. The cooler blood inside its tongue then gets pumped around the rest of its body.

Hippopotamuses spend most of their time in mud or water to keep cool.

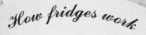
Fridges are built with plenty of insulation to stop warmth from the outside getting in, but they also have machinery that makes the inside cooler. If you look at the back of a fridge you will see a set of pipes, which feel warm. This warmth is the heat that has been taken from the inside of the fridge. The pipes go through to the inside of the fridge, too. The pipes contain a special liquid that evaporates easily. The fridge needs electricity to pump this liquid through the pipes. When the liquid gets inside the fridge, any warmth in the fridge heats it up enough to make it evaporate. As it evaporates, it absorbs the heat (just as sweat does when it evaporates). This gas travels through the pipes until it gets to the outside of the fridge. Outside the fridge the gas is compressed (squashed together) until it condenses (turns back into a liquid). When this happens, the heat that was absorbed inside the fridge is released. This is why the pipes at the back feel warm.

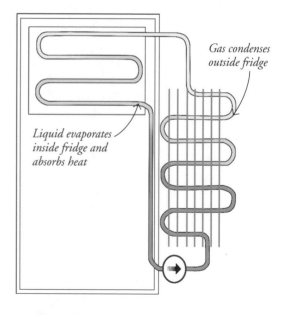

Gas condenses outside fridge

Liquid evaporates inside fridge and absorbs heat

THE COLD CHAIN

You probably think keeping things cold is important for storing food and to make you feel comfortable in hot weather, but it is very important in medicine, too.

Many medicines, including vaccines (which can stop diseases), have to be kept cold. If they are allowed to warm up at all, they will not work. When they are sent from the factories to the medical centers that use them, they follow a "cold chain." This means that they are kept at the right temperature.

These medicines are stored in fridges, and moved in refrigerated trucks or cool boxes. This can be difficult to do in developing countries. These countries are usually hot, and do not always have suitable vehicles. Clinics sometimes do not have an electricity supply to run fridges. One solution is to use their sunny climates to make solar-powered cool boxes—keeping medicines cool and patients alive.

Solar-powered cool boxes may be the answer to transporting vaccines in developing countries.

Insulated cool box

Solar panel collects sunlight

Charge controller regulates power to cool boxes

see for yourself

What is the best way of insulating an ice cube? Wrap up ice cubes in different ways. You could test insulation materials such as fleece, bubble wrap, paper, or plastic. Leave one of the ice cubes without any wrapping to see how much difference the insulation makes. Put them all in a warm place and see which one lasts the longest. Be sure to stand them on a plate to catch the water as they melt!

45 HOW TO SEE INSIDE YOUR BODY

Before a doctor can cure you, he or she needs to know what is wrong. If you have a problem with your skin it is fairly easy for a doctor to examine you and make a diagnosis. However, most health problems involve the inside of the body where it is more difficult to take a look.

ULTRASOUND SCANS

You cannot see the inside of your body because light waves cannot go through you. However sound waves can go through your body. This works best with ultrasounds, which are sounds that are too high for us to hear.

An ultrasound machine sends sound waves into the patient, and detects the echoes caused by the waves being reflected by the different parts of the patient. Ultrasound is used to look at unborn babies because the ultrasound waves do not harm the baby.

A substance that is neither an acid or an alkali is called a neutral substance. Water is a neutral substance.

Toothpaste is usually slightly alkaline. Acids in your mouth damage your teeth, and the alkali in toothpaste helps to neutralize these as you brush your teeth.
  Oven cleaners often contain alkalis, too —much stronger alkalis than you find in toothpaste!

Many colored chemicals change color when they are added to acids or alkalis. These substances are used as indicators, to detect whether something is an acid, an alkali, or neutral.

RED CABBAGE

You can make an indicator out of red cabbage. Take about half a cabbage and cut it up into small pieces. Put the pieces in a pan and pour enough boiling water over them to cover them. Boil the leaves for 5 to 10 minutes until the water has turned purple. Let it cool, then pour it through a sieve to remove the leaves. The purple liquid is your indicator.

Use your indicator to test substances around your home. Use a different small glass for each substance. Put a little of the substance in the glass and add a little indicator. Substances you can try include lemon juice, lemonade, window cleaner, detergent, and baking soda. Mix powders with a little water before testing them. If the indicator turns darker purple or red, your substance is an acid. If it turns blue, green, or yellow, then your substance is an alkali.

INDIGESTION

Your stomach contains quite strong hydrochloric acid. This helps to kill any microbes that may be on your food and is also needed to digest your food properly. Sometimes your stomach makes too much acid, and then you get indigestion. And sometimes this acid escapes upwards into your gullet (the tube that leads from your mouth to your stomach). This causes a pain called heartburn, although it has nothing to do with your heart! Indigestion tablets contain chemicals that neutralize acids. They become alkalis if you dissolve them in water. Neutralizing the extra acid helps to take away the pain.

ACID RAIN

Rainwater is naturally slightly acidic. This is because some of the carbon dioxide gas in the atmosphere dissolves in the rainwater to form an acid.

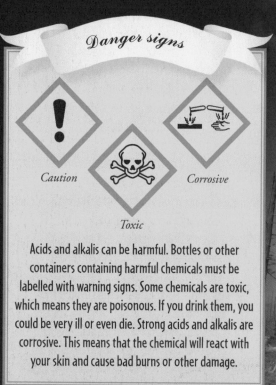

Danger signs

Caution

Toxic

Corrosive

Acids and alkalis can be harmful. Bottles or other containers containing harmful chemicals must be labelled with warning signs. Some chemicals are toxic, which means they are poisonous. If you drink them, you could be very ill or even die. Strong acids and alkalis are corrosive. This means that the chemical will react with your skin and cause bad burns or other damage.

Some of the gases that come out of cars and factory or power station chimneys contain other acidic chemicals that dissolve in rainwater.

This forms "acid rain," which is more acidic than normal rain. When it falls on lakes and rivers, it makes the water acidic, and this can kill fish and other living things. Acid rain falling onto forests can kill the trees.

Acid rain can be prevented by trapping these harmful gases before they escape into the atmosphere. This is being done in many countries, but acid rain is still a problem in many parts of the world.

NUMBER SCALE

Scientists can use indicators to find out if something is an acid or an alkali. Sometimes the indicator can also be used to say how strong or weak the acid or alkali is.

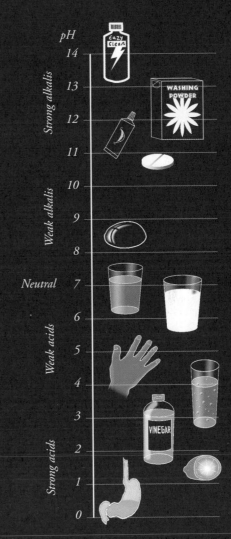

pH
14
13
12
11
10
9
8
7
6
5
4
3
2
1
0

Strong alkalis
Weak alkalis
Neutral
Weak acids
Strong acids

Acids that measure lower on the pH scale are stronger than those higher up. Anything measuring 7 is pH neutral.

Just saying "strong" or "weak" is not a very precise way of describing an acid. Scientists usually use the pH scale to describe acids and alkalis.

HOW TO VISIT ANOTHER STAR

Other than the Sun, the nearest star to the Earth is nearly 25,000,000,000,000 miles (40,000,000,000,000 km) away.
The Apollo spacecraft that went to the Moon would take more than 100 million years to get to the nearest star. So how can it be done?

FASTER ROCKETS

If we are to visit the stars, we will need to develop much faster rockets. We do not have the technology to build such rockets now, but we may do in the future. The first airplane flight was just over 100 years ago and flew only a few feet. Now some airplanes fly around the world without stopping—and some fly faster than the speed of sound! However, the journeys to the stars will still be very long, and there will be other problems to solve before reaching the stars will be possible.

ROCKET FUEL

The rockets that went to the Moon all those years ago carried all the fuel they needed with them, but a spacecraft going to a star would not be able to carry enough fuel to get there. One idea to solve this problem is to collect fuel on the way. There is some gas in space, although compared with the amount of gas in the Earth's atmosphere, space is almost empty! The gas found in space is mostly hydrogen, which can be used as rocket fuel.

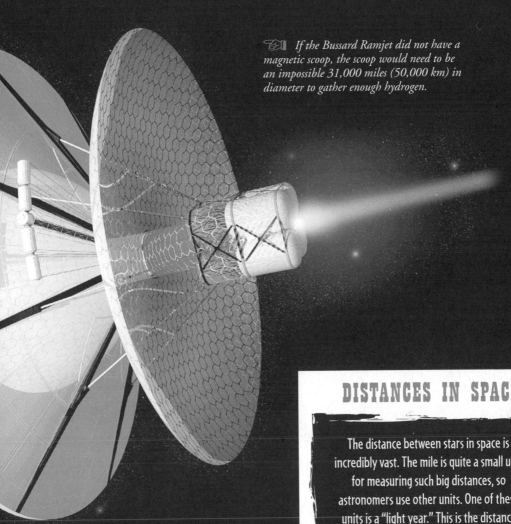

If the Bussard Ramjet did not have a magnetic scoop, the scoop would need to be an impossible 31,000 miles (50,000 km) in diameter to gather enough hydrogen.

The picture above shows a possible design for a "Bussard ramjet," which has a huge magnetic scoop at the front to gather up hydrogen as it travels.

DISTANCES IN SPACE

The distance between stars in space is incredibly vast. The mile is quite a small unit for measuring such big distances, so astronomers use other units. One of these units is a "light year." This is the distance that light will travel in one year, and is about 5,900,000,000,000 miles. That means our nearest star, Proxima Centauri, is about 4.2 light years from the Earth.

BUILDING THE SPACECRAFT

An interstellar spacecraft to carry people would have to be very, very big and heavy. If it is made strong enough to withstand the forces on it during launch from Earth, it would have to be even heavier, and launching it would be very difficult. Any future interstellar spacecraft will probably be built in space, using materials and parts launched from the Earth on much smaller rockets. It could even be built on the Moon, where gravity is much weaker than on Earth.

LIVING IN SPACE

The spacecraft would have to carry all the food, water, and oxygen that the crew would need for a journey that will last many years. You can read about some of the problems of space flight on page 110.

One way to provide oxygen and food could be to grow plants on the spacecraft. Plants do not need soil as long as they have water, light, and the correct nutrients.

Spacecraft of the future may have to be enormous to contain living quarters and enough supplies for interstellar journeys.

Once a spacecraft is moving it does not need to use its engines to keep going, as there is nothing in space to slow it down. However the quickest way to get to the stars would be to keep the engines running so that the spacecraft gets faster and faster. Then, when it is halfway there, the craft must turn so that its engines are pointing the other way. The engines must stay running to slow the spacecraft down again, otherwise it will just fly right past its destination.

Rocket accelerates (gets faster and faster) while its engine is working.

The rocket is still traveling towards the star, but it is slowing down because its engine is pointing the other way.

Growing plants without soil is called hydroponics. As plants grow they use carbon dioxide from the air and they release oxygen. The humans on the spacecraft will use this oxygen and release carbon dioxide again. Some of the plants can also be used for food.

OTHER IDEAS

There are lots of other ideas about interstellar travel, which you may have seen in science-fiction films. One of these is to make humans "hibernate" or to freeze them, so that they can go on very long journeys without getting any older. Another idea for very long trips is to have a "generation ship." This is a spacecraft that is big enough to carry between 100 and 200 people. Although the people will die before the end of the journey, they will have children and even grandchildren who will be alive when the ship reaches its final destination. These children will have to be trained to operate the spaceship to ensure a safe landing!

48 HOW TO SURVIVE A CAR CRASH

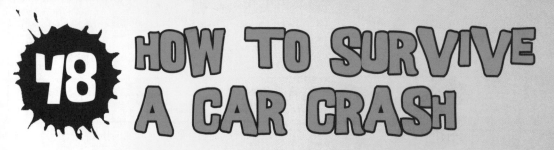

Nobody was seriously hurt in the car crash shown in the photograph, because it was made for a film. But you do not plan a real car crash, so how can you survive one?

THE EFFECTS OF SPEED

The best way to survive a car crash is not to have one in the first place! Speed makes a difference to how likely you are to have an accident. If you see a hazard ahead, it takes you longer to stop if you are going fast than if you are driving slowly. So the faster you are driving, the more space you should leave between your car and the car in front.

If you do have a crash, the faster you are going the worse the crash will be. If you accidentally drive into a wall or bridge at only a few miles per hour, the car will be damaged but you will not really feel it. Hit it at 50 mph (80 km/h) and, unless your car has very good safety features, you will be severely injured or killed.

A high-speed crash is more likely to cause injuries than a slow-speed fender-bender.

STOPPING DISTANCES

The stopping distance of a car is the distance it travels between the time the driver sees a hazard and the time it actually comes to a halt. If there is something closer to the car than the stopping distance, the car will hit it.

The thinking distance is how far the car travels while the driver is deciding to press the brake pedal. If the speed is doubled, the thinking distance is also doubled. If the driver is tired, the thinking distance is increased.

The braking distance is how far the car travels while the driver is pressing on the brakes. If you double your speed, the braking distance goes up four times. The braking distance also increases if the brakes are not working properly or if the tires do not have enough grip. Wet or icy conditions reduce grip because the friction between the tire and the road is reduced.

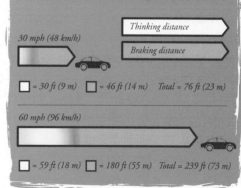

Thinking distance

Braking distance

30 mph (48 km/h)

☐ = 30 ft (9 m) ☐ = 46 ft (14 m) Total = 76 ft (23 m)

60 mph (96 km/h)

☐ = 59 ft (18 m) ☐ = 180 ft (55 m) Total = 239 ft (73 m)

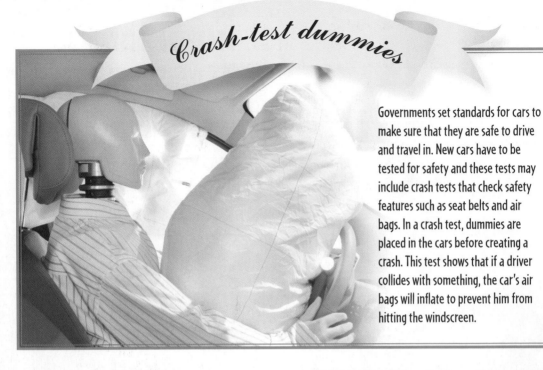

Governments set standards for cars to make sure that they are safe to drive and travel in. New cars have to be tested for safety and these tests may include crash tests that check safety features such as seat belts and air bags. In a crash test, dummies are placed in the cars before creating a crash. This test shows that if a driver collides with something, the car's air bags will inflate to prevent him from hitting the windscreen.

CRUMPLE ZONES

You will be injured in a crash if the forces on you are larger than your body can withstand. The size of the force depends on how quickly you stop. The more suddenly you stop, the bigger the forces on you. Modern cars are designed with "crumple zones." This means that the front of the car will crumple up if the car hits something. This absorbs some of the energy and means that the part of the car carrying the people does not slow down as quickly. This reduces the forces on the people in the car.

SEAT BELTS AND AIR BAGS

It is no use having a strong car if you do not stay in it to be protected. If the car rolls over in the crash and you are not wearing a seat belt, you could be thrown out of it. It is also no use having a car with crumple zones if you are not strapped in.

Passengers who are not wearing seat belts will carry on traveling forwards when the car slows down. They will stop only when they hit the dashboard or windscreen. Even with a seat belt on, your face could still hit the steering wheel or the front of the car in a crash. Modern cars also have air bags. These are like giant pillows that inflate if the car slows down very suddenly.

RALLY CARS

You can improve your chances of surviving a car crash by driving more slowly and wearing seat belts. Rally drivers and racing car drivers cannot go more slowly, and so are more likely to crash than normal road cars. To protect the driver and the co-driver if there is an accident or if the car rolls over, rally cars have an extra framework, called a roll cage, inside to make the whole car stronger. These drivers usually wear seat belts that go over both their shoulders, and they also wear crash helmets to protect their heads during an accident.

Lifting off the ground at high speed in a road car could be fatal but rally cars have additional safety features to ensure a safe landing.

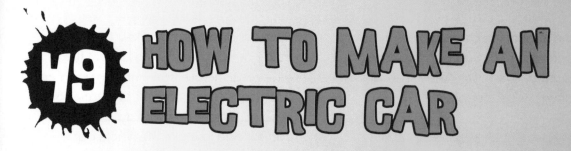

49 HOW TO MAKE AN ELECTRIC CAR

Solar-powered cars make electricity using sunshine and use the electricity to drive a motor to turn the wheels. However, they are not very practical for everyday use. They work only when the sun is shining!

WHAT IS A CAR?

For a scientist, a car is not just a box on four wheels that moves—it is an energy converter! Energy is needed for everything we do, and it has to be converted from one form to another. Most cars use gasoline or diesel. The fuel is a store of chemical energy. When the fuel is burned inside the engine, this chemical energy is converted to heat energy. The burning fuel produces gases, and the heat makes the gases expand. This pushes the pistons inside the engine and makes a shaft sticking out of the engine spin. This spinning shaft drives the wheels. The energy that was stored in the fuel is converted to kinetic (movement) energy.

ELECTRIC MOTORS

An electric car is also an energy converter. It converts chemical energy stored in a battery into electrical energy. The electrical energy is converted to movement energy in an electric motor.

A electric motor has a set of magnets that creates a magnetic field (you can read more about magnetic fields on page 155). It also has a coil of wire in the magnetic field. When an electric current flows in the coil of wire, the motor spins and is used to drive the car's wheels. If the size of the current is increased, the motor will go faster.

This solar-powered car has a top speed of 50 mph (80 km/h)—but there's only room for one person inside.

FUEL CELLS

Some buses and cars (above) use fuel cells instead of batteries to power their motors. A fuel cell combines hydrogen gas with oxygen to produce electricity—so they use hydrogen as a fuel. Gases take up a lot more space than liquids, so the hydrogen needs to be compressed into a strong fuel tank. Hydrogen also needs to be handled safely as it can explode if it escapes and mixes with air!

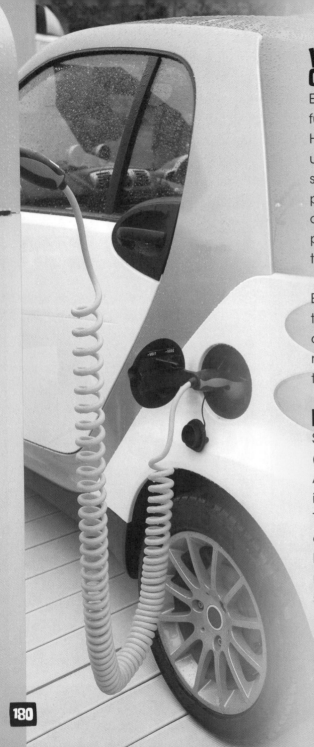

WHY ARE ELECTRIC CARS GOOD?

Electric cars do not produce exhaust fumes like diesel or gasoline cars do. However, they have to be charged up using electricity made in a power station, and the power station may produce pollution. But it is easier to clean up the gases coming from a power station than it is to clean up the exhaust fumes from cars.

Electric cars are also very quiet. In fact they are so quiet that manufacturers are thinking about making them noisier so that pedestrians can hear them coming!

PROBLEMS

Some cars can travel for 500 miles (800 km) before running out of fuel. An electric car does not use fuel, but it does need its battery to be charged. The best electric cars can go only about 93 miles (150 km) before their battery needs to be recharged. At the moment there are not many charging stations, so an electric car is only useful if you want to drive short distances. It also takes several hours to recharge a battery, but it takes a few minutes to fill the tank on a normal car.

Hybrid cars

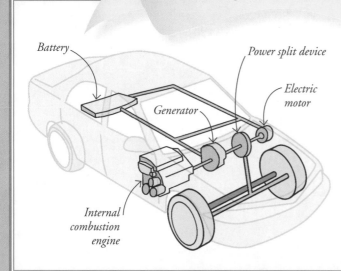

Battery

Power split device

Electric motor

Generator

Internal combustion engine

Hybrid cars have two engines—a normal gasoline engine and an electric motor. The car automatically switches between the different engines depending on how it is being driven. If the car is going fast then the gasoline engine is used. Gasoline engines waste a lot of energy when the car is going slowly, or if it has to keep stopping and starting in a town, so then the car switches to using the electric motor. This also helps to keep the air in towns and cities cleaner.

Engineers are working to develop better batteries that will allow cars to go much further without being too heavy, so we may see more electric cars in the future.

MAKING ELECTRICITY

Some electric cars can recharge their own batteries. An electric motor normally spins when an electric current is flowing through it. However if you make the motor spin, it will generate electricity. This is how generators in power stations work.

The brakes on a normal car work using friction. Pads are pressed against discs that are attached to the car's wheels, and friction makes the wheels slow down. Electric cars have brakes like this, but they can also have "regenerative braking." This is where the motor is switched off, and the car's movement is used to spin the motor. This slows down the car and produces electricity to recharge the battery.

An electric car cannot keep going for ever like this though—it can never make enough electricity while it is braking to make up for the electricity it uses while speeding up and keeping moving.

50 HOW TO LIVE ON ANOTHER PLANET

Humans and other animals and plants around us have evolved to live in the conditions on the Earth. The temperature and amount of rainfall varies from place to place, but there is always oxygen to breathe. People dream of being able to live on another planet, but how would we survive?

ARRIVING ON MARS

In the future, humans may be able to visit planets orbiting around other stars, but for now the most likely planet for humans to try to live on is Mars. Mars has an atmosphere, but it is thinner than the Earth's atmosphere and is mainly carbon dioxide. The first visits to Mars would last only a few months. Surviving on Mars for this length of time would be very similar to surviving in a spacecraft (you can read about surviving in space on page 110). If humans wanted to live on Mars for longer periods, they could build a large dome to hold air. They would not need to wear spacesuits or breathing masks in the dome. They would be able to grow crops, which would also help to recycle the carbon dioxide that they breathed out. The dome would have to be strong enough to withstand the pressure of the air inside it and to resist damage from Martian sandstorms.

This is an artist's impression of what the future on Mars might be like.

BIOSPHERE 2

Some scientists are investigating how to solve some of the problems of living on other planets. One investigation was in Biosphere 2, a huge building in the Arizona desert. This was built to test ideas about living in closed systems, such as a dome on another planet. The building was sealed, and contained all the plants and animals that eight people would need to live there for two years. It was not a total success, as some of the animals and most of the insects died, but the scientists did manage to grow all their own food and stay healthy.

Jupiter's moon, Ganymede, is the largest moon in the solar system. It is thought to have a saltwater ocean under its surface.

TERRAFORMING MARS

Terraforming means doing things to another planet to make the conditions more like those on the Earth. To terraform Mars we would need to make it warmer, make the atmosphere thicker, and make sure it contains enough oxygen for us to breathe. Extra water could also be added to Mars if comets could be brought from the outer solar system. These would melt on Mars and would also provide gases to make the atmosphere thicker. The gases would include "greenhouse" gases that would trap heat. As Mars warmed up, frozen water beneath its surface would melt. Eventually conditions might be right for plants to grow, and they would add oxygen to the atmosphere.

WHERE ELSE COULD WE LIVE?

Mars is the only planet in the solar system that humans could live on, other than the Earth. Venus is a similar size to the Earth and has similar gravity, but it has a very thick atmosphere made mostly of carbon dioxide. The surface of Venus is very hot—up to 860°F (460°C) and the rain is made of sulphuric acid! Mercury is too hot because it is very close to the Sun. The planets beyond Mars (Jupiter, Saturn, Uranus, and Neptune) are gas giants. If they do have a solid surface it is far below the top of the atmosphere that we can see, and the gravity would be far too strong for humans to survive.

The gas giant planets do have a lot of moons, and one day it might be possible for humans to visit these. These moons are very cold, because the gas giant planets are so far from the Sun, so humans would not be able to terraform them. To live on one of these moons, we would have to live inside domes or dig enormous underground shelters.

Terrarium building

A terrarium (or bottle garden) is a bit like a dome on another planet—once it is set up, the plants in it should grow without any water or air being added. To make a bottle garden you need a large, clean glass bottle with a wide neck, a stopper for the bottle, some clean pebbles or gravel, potting soil, paper to make a funnel, and a couple of long sticks. You also need some small, slow-growing plants—ask a gardener or garden center for advice.

1. Put a layer of pebbles in the bottom of the bottle. Use the funnel to add potting soil on top so that the sides of the bottle do not get dirty.

2. Use the sticks to make holes in the soil and put in your plants.

3. Wet the soil and put the stopper on.

Leave your bottle garden somewhere light, but not in direct sunlight. If you see a lot of condensation on the inside of the glass you have too much water in it, so take the stopper off for a while. If there is no condensation you do not have enough water so add a bit more. After you have made some adjustments like this, you should be able to leave the stopper on permanently.

GLOSSARY

AIR PURIFIERS
Special devices or machines that are used to clean the air.

AIR RESISTANCE
The force of the air that acts on objects to slow them down.

BODY LANGUAGE
Showing your feelings by the way you stand or walk, and by the expression on your face.

CAMOUFLAGE
A way of hiding things to make them look as if they are part of their surroundings.

COLONIES
Groups of animals living together in an organized system or way. Ants and meerkats live in colonies.

CROSS-TRAINING
To train to be good at different, but related, sports. For example, sportspeople who run may take up cycling as part of their training program.

DENSITY
The amount of mass in a substance.

ECHOLOCATION
The system used by animals, such as dolphins and bats, boats and submarines to detect and locate objects. The animals do this by emitting high-pitched sounds that reflect off the object and return to the animal's ears.

EXPEDITION
A trip or journey with a specific purpose or goal.

FORCE
Something that acts to change the speed or direction of movement of a body, or its shape.

FORENSIC SCIENTISTS
Scientists who use scientific evidence to solve crimes.

FRICTION
The resistance to movement that occurs when two objects are in contact.

GRAVITY
The force of attraction between objects. On Earth, gravity causes things to fall towards the center of the Earth.

INDIGESTION
An uncomfortable feeling when there is too much acid in the stomach.

INFRARED
A type of light that you feel as heat, but cannot see.

INSULATION
The covering that surrounds an object to reduce the transfer of heat.

MICRO-ORGANISMS
An organism that is so small it can be seen only by using a microscope.

NUCLEAR POWER
Electricity generated by a nuclear reactor.

NYLON
A light and strong artificial fiber that can be woven into cloth.

ORBIT
The path followed by an object in space

ORGAN TRANSPLANT
An operation where an organ, such as a heart, kidney, or liver, is taken out of one person and put into another ill person to save the ill person's life.

QUARRY
A pit, usually open to the air, from which building stone or slate is obtained.

REFLECT
To bounce off, for example when rays of light reflect off a mirror, or sound echoes reflect off a solid object.

RESOURCES
Things that can be used, for example water, metals, or fuel.

SPECIES
A group of plants or animals that are very similar and can breed to produce new offspring.

ULTRAVIOLET
Light that has a wavelength shorter than visible light but longer than X-rays.

VENOM
Something that is harmful if taken into

INDEX

indigestion 168
infrared light 86–89
insects 26, 29, 93
instinct 83
insulation 112, 158–161
intelligence 76–77
internet 142
Inuit people 48–49
irrigation 92, 93
IVF 132

J K

joints 78–79, 115
keeping cool 158–159
kinetic energy 178

L

lactic acid 80, 81
lahars 42
lava 40–42, 46
lift 119, 148
light 10, 34, 58, 60, 86–88,
    138–139
light years 171
lightning 54–57, 154
lightning conductors 56
limestone 43, 45
long life 38–39

M

magma 40–42, 46
magnetic fields 155–157, 164,
    179
Mars 182–185
meat 93
medicines 151
memory 77, 83, 133
Mercury 185
meteorites 52–53, 105, 137,
    145

microscopes 165
migration 156–157
military vehicles 37
mimicry 37
mind reading 20–23
mines 104–105
mirages 138–139
mirrors 10–11
money, forged 140–141
monsoons 74
moons 63, 184, 185
mountaineering 30–33
mountains 74
MRI scans 164, 165
mudflows 42
muscles 78–81, 113, 114
musical instruments 94–97

N

Neptune 62
Newton, Isaac 65
night vision 88
Nobel, Alfred 135
North Pole 49, 50
nuclear power 19
nutrients 91

O

ocean depths 58–61
optical fibers 163
orchestras 96
organs 130–131, 133
oxygen 31, 32, 33, 80, 110,
    172–173, 184–185
ozone 124

P

paint 27, 142
parachutes 66–69
pathology 26–27, 165

periscopes 11
pesticides 91, 92–93
petrol 135, 182
pH scale 169
pheromones 82–84
pitch 95
plagiarism 142
planets 62–65, 105, 182–185
plants 28, 29, 73, 91, 100–101,
    147, 172–173, 185
polar bears 9, 50, 147
pollen 26, 29
pollution 144, 147, 180
population 90
power stations 98–101, 180
prisms 86, 139
protein 81

R

rain 72–75, 92, 147
    acid rain 168–169
rainbows 138–139
rally cars 177
refraction 138–139
retina 87
rigor mortis 27
robots 114–117
rockets 149–150, 170
rocks 45–47, 53, 105
rowing boats 16–17

S

Sahara Desert 74
sailing ships 18
salamanders 133
salt 93, 124–125
Sami people 48, 49
Saturn 62
scent 84, 85
Scott, Robert 123, 125

CONTENTS

INTRODUCTION

WHO BROKE INTO the jewelry store? Unfortunately, the thief didn't leave a card at the scene of the crime with a name and contact info. But maybe he or she left something behind that will be just as helpful: DNA evidence.

There are many different kinds of clues that come into play in a criminal investigation: evidence from eyewitnesses, security-camera video, and fingerprints, to name just a few. But sometimes those things are unreliable, or inconclusive, or simply not available. When that's the case, the detective might turn to a tool that's expensive but often more useful: DNA identification.

But what exactly *is* DNA, and how can it solve crimes?

BUILDING BLOCK BASICS

DNA STANDS FOR A WORD so long that even scientists don't bother pronouncing it: deoxyribonucleic acid.

In the center of almost every cell in our bodies, there's a piece of DNA, designed to give the body instructions. In human DNA, those instructions say things like: "Create two legs, two arms, two eyes, and one nose." In a lemur's DNA, there are blueprints for a long, striped tail. A rainbow trout's DNA includes a recipe for iridescent scales.

All the instructions to create a person are written in a code about 3 billion units long. And the entire thing has to fit inside the center of a cell.

Which seems impossible! How can so much information be squeezed into such a tiny space?

Well, each DNA molecule is shaped like a spring. Imagine a toy Slinky. If you stretch it out, it might be taller than you are. But when you let it go, it's smaller than your hand. DNA molecules are like microscopic Slinkies. They're twisted so tightly that they can fit inside your cells. But if you took all those spring shapes from your body, joined them, and stretched them, they'd reach to the moon and back . . . six thousand times!

Our DNA molecules are actually double springs, connected by rungs, so that they can carry even more information. They're shaped a lot like spiral staircases. The twisting "handrails" are made of sugar (deoxyribose) and phosphate. The "stairs" are made of four chemical bases called nucleotides: adenine, guanine, cytosine, and thymine. Those chemical names are a mouthful, so everyone calls them by their initials: A, G, C, and T.

Each person's DNA is unique. Yours might make your eyes blue instead of brown. Other pieces might give you extra-fast reflexes, or strange and wiggly ears. It all depends on your own particular code.

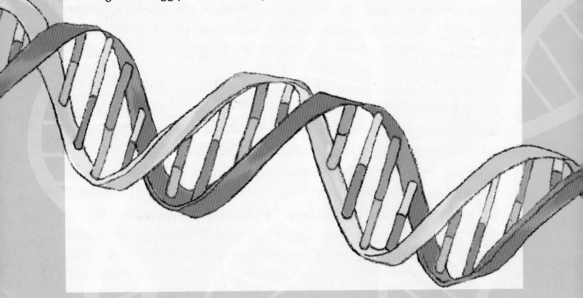

DNA FINGERPRINTS

YOUR DNA and the DNA of your best friend are remarkably similar. In fact, they're 99.9 percent the same. That explains why you both have hair on the top of your head, two eyebrows, two eyes, one nose, and a mouth. But unless you're identical twins, your DNA also has a few pretty obvious differences. You each have 3 billion units of code, after all. So even if only 0.1 percent is different, that's still 3 million units. It's as if each human on earth has a unique barcode.

Parts of the DNA code repeat over and over again, in a pattern. Scientists can look at the patterns and tell which people are related to one another. The repeating patterns of family members, who share a lot of the same DNA, are similar, while those of strangers are usually quite different.

How does this help in a criminal investigation? Well, if crime scene investigators can find even a few cells—in a drop of spit, a single hair, or a smear of blood, for example—they can send the evidence to a lab, where researchers look at the repeating patterns. They enter those patterns into a computer and compare them to the DNA patterns of a suspect. It's like using a high-tech fingerprint to identify a criminal.

Sometimes, evidence hides in unusual places. Detectives have found DNA on the handles of base-ball bats, the licked surfaces of postage stamps, the tips of toothpicks, and the rims of drinking glasses.

SUPER SLEUTH ①

FOR THOUSANDS OF YEARS, humans have understood that traits are passed down through families. Ancient farmers bred their biggest, strongest animals to create big, strong offspring. They knew that by planting the kernels of the tallest, healthiest corn, they were likely to get better crops the following year. And they recognized that two parents with big noses were more likely to have a big-nosed kid.

But they didn't know *why* this was true.

Ancient philosophers took their best guesses:

- SEEDS More than two thousand years ago, a guy named Hippocrates suggested that both men and women produced tiny seeds, which joined to create babies.

- GUTS The Greek philosopher Aristotle said women provided the blood and guts of babies, but men gave them their shape.

- SPIRIT In China, early doctors believed that both mother and father contributed a sort of life energy to create a baby.

There was no way to prove or disprove any of these ideas until the 1600s, when microscopes were invented. Finally, doctors and scientists could see individual cells. They discovered the egg cells of women and the sperm cells of men. And they thought that maybe—just maybe—these cells helped make babies.

So, did they conclude that sperm and egg united, each providing genetic material to the new creature?

No. They spent the next two hundred years arguing. One group of scientists said that the sperm was responsible for a baby's creation, while others insisted that it was the egg.

It seems a bit silly now, but there were good reasons for all this confusion. Sometimes babies looked exactly like their fathers. Sometimes they looked like their mothers. Sometimes people passed crooked ears or funny chins on to their children, and sometimes they didn't. Sometimes a baby was born with disabilities that didn't seem to come from its father or mother. The evidence was a mess!

Fortunately, in the mid-1700s, two men took some important steps toward understanding it all:

- In England, a sheep breeder named Robert Bakewell set out to turn a better profit from barnyard animals. He bred not simply for

strong and healthy animals, but also for those with specific traits that would be valuable in the marketplace. Eventually, he produced sheep with long and shiny wool, meaty bodies, and no sharp horns.

- In France, a mathematician named Pierre Louis Maupertuis traced members of a Berlin family born with extra fingers. Sometimes the trait seemed to be passed from the father, and sometimes from the mother. So Maupertuis suggested that both parents contributed "hereditary particles" to their babies.

Today, the conclusions of these men seem obvious. But that's because we've all grown up with the idea that we inherit Mom's eyes, Dad's nose, and Grandma's temper. In the 1700s, these were significant steps toward understanding genetics.

Spanish royalty from the House of Habsburg had no trouble recognizing a family member in a portrait. Because their intermarrying led to DNA trouble, family members inherited the very prominent "Habsburg jaw". The jaw of King Charles II was so large, his top and bottom teeth didn't meet. He had serious chewing and speaking problems.

BAD BLOOD

BY THE 1800s, people understood that diseases and disorders were sometimes passed on along family lines. The most obvious example in Europe was a condition often called "the royal disease." It was hemophilia, a disorder in which blood doesn't clot properly. People with hemophilia bruise easily and can bleed to death if they're cut or badly bumped. And while females carry the disease, it's usually males who show symptoms.

In Europe, it was several *royal* males.

Queen Victoria had unknowingly passed hemophilia to some of her children, who then passed it to their children. Because the princes and princesses of England married other nobles, the disease spread through the royal families of England, Spain, Germany, and Russia, wreaking havoc along the way. One of Queen Victoria's sons, two grandsons, and six great-grandsons died of the disorder.

People didn't understand exactly how the disease was transmitted, but they knew it passed from parent to child.

ISLAND HOPPING

IDEAS ABOUT HEREDITY began to grow more specific when a young naturalist named Charles Darwin hitched a ride on a boat bound for South America. In 1831, the *Beagle* set sail from England. It would take Charles to the Amazon rainforest, the cliffs of Argentina, and eventually along the equator to the Galápagos Islands, about 970 kilometers (600 miles) west of Ecuador.

Formed by volcanoes rising from the sea, these islands were so far from land that the plants and animals there developed differently from their mainland counterparts. Over thousands of years, they became entirely unique. The islands themselves—eighteen main ones, and several smaller outcroppings—were separated by deep channels that few animals could cross. Charles learned that locals could tell from which island a tortoise came just by looking at the pattern on its shell.

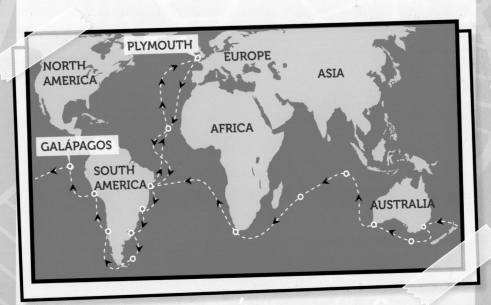

Excited by the variety of unusual creatures, Charles began collecting specimens. He took fish, snails, birds, reptiles, and bugs, labeling them and packing them for transport. By the time he headed back to England in 1836, he had 1,750 pages of notes and more than five thousand biological bits, from feathers to bones. He had everything he needed to—eventually—figure out why and how certain genetic traits were passed along family lines.

BIRDS OF A FEATHER

HOW COULD ONE MAN EXAMINE five thousand samples? There was no way Charles Darwin could get through all that work alone. So he bundled up some of his specimens and sent them off to other experts.

Among his collections were several birds—some with small beaks and some with sharp ones, some found in trees and some found on the

ground. He guessed that these specimens included blackbirds, grosbeaks, and finches. They weren't the most interesting or the most beautiful of his creatures, so Charles sent them to a bird expert to study. When the expert wrote back to Charles, he said, thanks for all these birds, but they're not really as different as you said they were. They're all various species of finch.

What? All the birds turned out to be members of the same feathered club! How could they look so different if they all had common ancestors? Suddenly, Charles had an idea. Maybe he'd collected each bird from a separate island. Maybe the finches that lived in different environments had specific traits, the same way the tortoises from different islands had unique shells.

Soon, Charles came up with some theories about how animals evolved to suit their environments. But he wasn't yet ready to share his ideas with the world.

Instead, he bought himself a whole lot of pigeons. He joined pigeon clubs and built a pigeon house and wrote to pigeon experts. Why? Well, partly because he fell in love with the amazing variations in the pigeon world. But also because he wanted to prove that the main breeds had all descended from the plain old

DID YA HEAR THAT?
I'M AMAZING!

rock pigeon. He showed that by breeding some birds for color, farmers had produced one species; by breeding them for size, they'd produced another. And so on, and so on.

Charles started with the knowledge that birds inherited traits from their parents and could pass those traits to their offspring. He then connected that idea to his Galápagos research. In the wild, creatures with certain traits were more likely to survive in a specific environment. A finch with a large beak, for example, might be better at cracking nuts. If nuts were the main source of food on an island, then that finch would grow stronger and healthier, have more babies than weaker finches, and pass on its strong beak. Eventually, strong-beaked finches could take over an island.

When he published his book *On the Origin of Species* in 1859, Charles gave this idea a name: *natural selection*. Stronger creatures lived longer and passed on their traits more often.

But he worried that this might not be easily understood, so he borrowed another phrase from a fellow scientist, Herbert Spencer: *survival of the fittest.* The creatures with traits that best "fit" their environments were the strongest. They survived, and passed on their useful traits to the next generation, while others died out.

In all of his research, Charles was exploring genetics. But he still didn't know why traits were sometimes inherited and sometimes not. And where in the body did instructions for a trait live? How, exactly, did a creature pass on a characteristic to its young? For answers to those questions, the world would have to wait.

Today, the Galápagos Islands are part of a national park in Ecuador. To help protect the creatures there, the government allows only a limited number of visitors.

DEVILS AND DETAILS

IN THE MID-1800s, Charles Darwin and other scientists like him were beginning to understand two things. First, that different creatures were uniquely suited to their environments. Second, that diversity—all sorts of animals, each a little bit different—equaled strength. If there were some animals better adapted to cold, then those creatures would survive unusually chilly winters. If some birds were better suited to eating nuts, they could live through seasons with little fruit. And those better-adapted animals would help to keep the whole species from dying out during hard times.

These theories help explain a lot. But they're no help to the Tasmanian devil. About forty thousand years ago, Tasmanian devils lived across Australia. Then the aboriginal people arrived on the continent. With them came wild dogs called dingoes—a new predator. Hunted by dingoes, the devils soon died out. Except on the island of Tasmania.

Tasmania is separated from the mainland of Australia by a wide, deep channel. No one knows exactly how the devils got to the island. And not many made it there. Probably all 150,000 of the animals still living descended from just a few individual ancestors. And because of that, the entire living population is genetically pretty similar.

That genetic similarity is now causing problems. A contagious cancer has attacked the animals, invading their mouths and making it impossible for them to eat.

If the devils were a normal group of animals, each creature would have a wide variety of different, unique genes, some of which might resist the cancer. But the devils share most of the same genes. So, one after another, the animals are dying. Almost two-thirds of them are gone. The species faces extinction.

Not if scientists can help it, though.

Today, wildlife officials are capturing healthy Tasmanian devils and keeping them separate from the wild population to help ensure some of the animals escape the disease. Other scientists are trying to figure out if a few devils might be genetically resistant. If they can find even a small number of animals able to fight off the cancer, they can breed more tumor-resistant devils. It's a small chance, but one that scientists are determined to pursue.

In the meantime, Australian biologists are sending a warning to wildlife officials in other parts of the world: Make sure you have big populations of animals, with lots of genetic diversity. That's the only way wild creatures can be safe from unexpected threats.

CREATURE FEATURES

TAKE A LOOK AROUND YOUR CLASSROOM, or around a local restaurant. There are lots of variations in any handful of people. Even within our families, most of us are a mishmash of features. Maybe your great-aunt says you have your father's nose, or Grandma says you're the spitting image of your mother. Or maybe you have green eyes when both your parents have brown. Our insides are just as variable. Some of us have better immune systems, some of us have larger hearts, and some of us have different wiring in tiny areas of our brains.

So, we know that each of us is an assortment of parts. But how are our traits passed along from one generation to the next? The man who finally figured it out didn't work on something as complicated as people. He studied pea plants. Thousands and thousands of pea plants.

GREGOR THE GARDENER

YOU'RE AN ANXIOUS, INTROVERTED BRAINIAC. All you want to do is study. But your farming family can't afford to pay for much education. Should you:

- ☑ Work as a gardening beekeeper to support yourself?

- ☑ Spend your sister's dowry on science classes?

- ☑ Join the priesthood?

IF YOU ARE GREGOR MENDEL, THE ANSWER IS: ALL OF THE ABOVE.

After spending every cent on schooling and still not getting his fill, Gregor donned monk's robes in 1843. He then dove into studies of math, physics, and botany.

In 1865, he took the same determination he'd applied to his education and started breeding simple, fast-growing pea plants. He soon figured out that plants inherited traits from their parent plants, and that each trait was passed along separately. For example, a parent plant might have yellow seeds and large leaves. It could pass either or both of these traits along to the next generation. Each trait was like a separate building block that could be used or not used.

Eventually, after studying thousands of plants, Gregor came up with two basic rules:

RULE #1: THE LAW OF SEGREGATION For every trait, we inherit two possibilities, one from the female side and one from the male side. Some of these possibilities are "dominant" and others are "recessive." The dominant possibilities are the ones we are most likely to inherit.

In Mendel's pea plants, there were two possibilities for seed color: yellow or green. Yellow was the dominant color. A plant that inherited yellow from both the male and female sides would certainly produce yellow seeds. A plant that inherited yellow from the male side and green from the female side would still have yellow seeds, because yellow was dominant. It trumped green. But if a plant inherited green from the male side and green from the female side, then the recessive trait would win and the seed color would be green.

RULE #2: THE LAW OF INDEPENDENT ASSORTMENT Different traits can be passed on independently. So, a pea plant could inherit the green leaves of one parent plant without necessarily inheriting its yellow seeds.

Gregor was also sure that inheritance could be predicted with mathematical rules. Today's scientists think he might have made his results a little more regular than they really were, just to fit his perfect math equations. Still, he was on the right track. He set out to share his findings with the world.

First he published his results. There was no response. Then he presented his research to other scientists, and asked others to try the same experiments. No one seemed interested. After years of work, poor Gregor discovered that no one cared about his discoveries. Then he was elected the abbot of his monastery and had no more time for science anyway. He died in 1884 without having found anyone to pursue his ideas about inherited traits. In fact, his research seemed so useless that the other monks burned his notebooks.

Maybe the world just wasn't ready.

THE LIGHT BULB GOES ON

SIXTEEN YEARS AFTER MENDEL'S DEATH, three other scientists working on separate plant experiments each discovered that plants passed different traits to their offspring independently. When they searched through old science journals, wondering if anyone had looked into this before, they rediscovered Gregor Mendel.

Suddenly, Gregor's old discoveries were big news. And there were more researchers making other discoveries, all pointing the way toward DNA:

- In the 1860s, Swiss doctor Friedrich Miescher studied white blood cells. Inside the center of each cell, the nucleus, he found a chemical goo he called *nuclein*. What he was actually seeing was DNA, though it would be decades before anyone had the powerful tools needed to truly see the molecule's form.

- A Dutch botanist named Hugo de Vries did much of the same research Gregor did, without knowing about Gregor's work. But Hugo didn't conclude that species inherited traits in an orderly, mathematical way. After studying evening primroses, he thought that new species arose through big, sudden mutations. Hugo was wrong with that particular theory, but his work sparked lots of new ideas about inheritance.

- In 1919, a Russian biochemist named Phoebus Levene figured out which chemicals joined together to form DNA.

Slowly, with each new discovery, the world was growing closer to understanding how microscopic codes could hold the instructions for all life.

Where did Friedrich Miescher get his supply of white blood cells?

He scraped the pus from used bandages!

THE SUSPECTS

DEE ZASTER
CASHIER

RUSTY HAMMER
CASHIER

**TERRY BILL
CONVICTED THIEF**

CAMMIE SOLE
STORE MANAGER

DR. HACKER, DENTIST
REGULAR CUSTOMER

ELLA VADER
LOCAL SECURITY GUARD

STAN STILL
SALES REPRESENTATIVE

DAISY PICKER
OWNS THE STORE NEXT DOOR

DWAYNE PIPE
CUSTODIAN

PIA NUTT
SUPERMODEL,
REGULAR CUSTOMER

HAZEL NUTT
SUPERMODEL,
REGULAR CUSTOMER

IDA GOTTAWAY
STORE BOOKKEEPER

WHERE SHOULD THE INVESTIGATION GO FROM HERE?

HINT: The detective has a DNA "fingerprint" from the glove. What will she need from the suspects?

Answer: A DNA sample

CLUE 2 COLLECTING

IF YOU INHERIT your dad's big ears, you might say, "They're in my genes" or "Big ears are in my DNA." To most of us, those sentences mean pretty much the same thing. Scientifically, though, genes and DNA are at different levels of the same life-building system. There's another level, too, called the chromosome. From smallest to largest, here's what these terms mean:

SMALLEST: DNA DNA molecules are those double springs that look like two handrails (made of sugar and phosphate) connected by nucleotide "stairs" (A, G, C, and T). The DNA molecule provides the code for building the body.

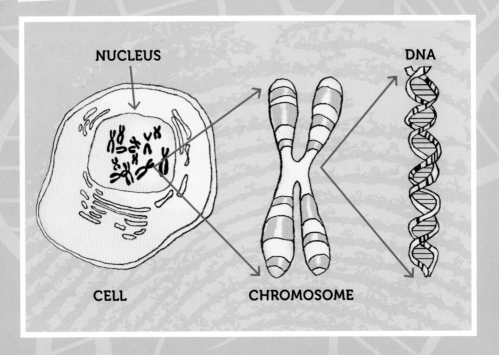

NUCLEUS

DNA

CELL

CHROMOSOME

BIGGER: GENES Genes are snippets or chunks of DNA that carry the building instructions for our different parts. Traits are passed on from parents to children by the work of genes.

BIGGEST: CHROMOSOMES Chromosomes are long strings of DNA molecules wrapped around proteins. Each chromosome contains many genes. Humans have forty-six chromosomes, arranged in pairs.

Where do you find DNA, genes, and chromosomes? If you look at a single cell under a powerful microscope, you'll see a dark spot in the center. That's the nucleus. It's your cell's miniature brain, or command center.

Are you thinking small? Think even smaller! You need a microscope to see a single cell. Then you need an even more powerful microscope to see inside the nucleus. And there probably isn't a microscope at your school that's powerful enough to clearly see a DNA molecule.

MASH-UPS AND MIX-UPS

CELLS MAKE NEW CELLS BY DIVIDING, and every time a cell divides in two, it has to pass its exact DNA code on to the new cell. Now, imagine if someone gave you a code and asked you to handwrite a copy. If it were a page or two long, no problem. But what if the code had 3 *billion* letters, like the units of code in a cell's DNA? You'd probably make a few mistakes along the way.

Cells divide inside you millions of times each day. So it's no surprise that every once in a while something gets copied a little differently from how it should.

Usually, there are extras of every instruction, which act as insurance against errors. If one tiny chunk of DNA instructs your body to have two eyes, for example, other chunks repeat those instructions. Those repeated codes are in places where your body can double-check itself, to make sure you don't end up with three eyes by accident.

But even with extra checks and double instructions, mistakes still happen. Every once in a while, a major mix-up gets through the system and a mutation occurs. A mutation is a change in the DNA pattern that wasn't supposed to happen.

Mutations can cause all sorts of wild and wonderful things . . .

ALIEN ISLAND

MORE THAN 15 MILLION YEARS AGO, the shoreline of what is now Yemen shifted, and a few pieces of the mainland were pulled farther and farther into the Indian Ocean. They survived as the island of Socotra and three smaller outcroppings nearby.

When it was ripped from the mainland, Socotra took its plants and animals with it. But over millions of years, those plants and animals evolved separately from the ancestors they'd left behind. Eventually, Socotra began to look different from anywhere else on earth. Between the island's desert bowls, mountains, and beaches grew plants that seemed like alien species, and animals that early explorers couldn't identify.

In the 1990s, the United Nations sent a team of researchers to catalog all the plants and animals on the island. They found seven hundred species different from those anywhere else on earth. Those seven hundred species have DNA that changed, over centuries and centuries, until its instructions created entirely unique creatures.

Here are descriptions of just a few of Socotra's otherworldly inhabitants:

- The dragon's blood tree, named for its red sap, has branches that reach up to suck moisture from the island's mountain mists.

- The Chamaeleo monachus has a long, patterned tail and thin, agile limbs. According to local lore, those who hear this lizard's hiss lose their ability to talk.

- Like a shrub from a Dr. Seuss book, the desert rose has a thick trunk to anchor itself to Socotra's rocky cliffs, and hot-pink flowers to attract local pollinating insects.

A rose is a rose, except in Socotra.

Dragon's blood trees evolved over thousands of years. But climate change means temperatures are rising by the decade. Without as much moisture in Socotra's mists, fewer young trees can survive on the rocks. Researchers worry the plant won't adapt quickly enough to survive.

The differences that make these species unique began as random DNA mutations. In some cases, the mutations were just plain mistakes. They weren't particularly helpful, but they weren't damaging either. Other mutations helped the plants and animals survive on their island home. The desert rose, for example, began as an ordinary plant that blooms throughout the region. But on Socotra, the DNA of a few plants said, "Grow bigger." These larger plants were better able to withstand the island's monsoon winds. As more of the big plants survived, passing their DNA to their offspring, the smaller plants died out. And over all those millions of years, the giant desert rose of Socotra kept changing, adapting to its environment, until it became a unique species all its own.

What scientists have seen on Socotra is similar to what Charles Darwin observed in the Galápagos Islands back in the 1830s. There, again over millions of years, plants and animals experienced a lot of random DNA mutations. When the mutations provided an advantage—like a change to the shape of a bird's beak that made it easier to get food—that new trait made it more likely that the plant or animal would survive, and pass that trait on through DNA to the next generation. The plants that were best adapted to the living conditions on the islands and the creatures best able to find food and water and mates eventually took over. This is what Charles called "survival of the fittest."

Places with plentiful food and water support a diversity of plants and animals—even the weaker ones sometimes thrive. But in harsh places, only the creatures most suited to the environment manage to survive.

GENETICS ROCK STAR

GRASSHOPPER GAMES

BY THE EARLY 1900s, scientists had pretty much agreed that traits were inherited. But they were still arguing about *how* those traits were passed from parent to child. There were two main theories:

- Darwin's right! Random changes are happening constantly. The most helpful traits survive while others die out.

- No, Mendel's right! Traits are passed along by regular, predictable systems, according to which traits are dominant and which are recessive.

Before they could decide who was right, researchers needed more information about what happens inside cells. The first to contribute some of that knowledge was a farm boy from the wheat fields of Kansas.

Walter Sutton looked as if he belonged tossing hay bales. He was six feet tall and weighed more than two hundred pounds. But when his little brother died of typhoid fever, Walter embarked on a career in medicine and research.

Some of his early research endeavors still involved the farm. His first published paper was based on the study of the grasshoppers he found in his dad's fields. But Walter went on to study all sorts of creatures, and all sorts of cells. Collaborating with a researcher named E. B. Wilson, he began focusing on heredity. Soon he had solved some huge genetic puzzles. In 1902, he offered major conclusions, including:

- Chromosomes contain genes that provide the code for passing on traits.
- Our chromosomes are organized in mother-father pairs. We get half our chromosomes from our mothers and half from our fathers.
- The chromosomes we're born with are the ones we keep for our whole lives.

Walter learned more than ever before about how traits are passed along, and he also explained how we humans inherit some of our traits from our mothers and some from our fathers. The chromosomes in the centers of our cells are the vehicles for that inheritance.

Y SO DIFFERENT?

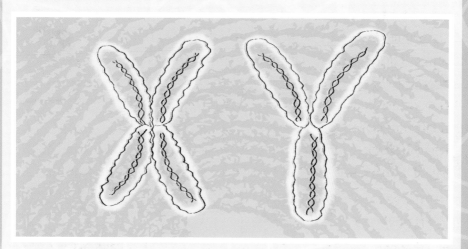

HUMANS INHERIT twenty-three pairs of chromosomes from their parents. And most of those pairs are logical and orderly. Only one pair stands out.

Imagine a baby shower, where twenty-two relatives contribute perfectly matching little clothes. A blue shirt and blue pants. A green shirt and green pants. Then one strange relative turns up and gives a purple shirt with orange shorts—something completely different from the other gifts. Something that doesn't match at all!

In the human body, that unmatched set is the twenty-third chromosome pair—and that pair determines whether a baby is a boy or a girl. In a girl, the two chromosomes in the pair are both X-shaped. In a boy, there is one X-shaped chromosome and one small, mismatched Y-shaped chromosome.

But that strange Y has unusual power. One gene on that Y chromosome, called "sex-determining region Y" (SRY), builds a protein that communicates with the other chromosomes to trigger male development.

When you were a tiny embryo inside your mother's womb, you were neither boy nor girl. Not yet. You had tiny reproductive parts that could become either ovaries (in a girl) or testes (in a boy).

If you're a boy, then something changed at the six-week stage. Your SRY gene began to produce proteins. And those proteins instructed your body to become male. If you're a girl, you didn't have a Y chromosome, so you didn't have an SRY gene. Your body didn't make those special proteins, and the embryo developed into a female.

That's right—humans become male or female based only on the activities of one tiny gene and its army of proteins.

FLY GUYS

AT THE BEGINNING of the twentieth century, Thomas Hunt Morgan worried that science was on the wrong track. He questioned everything. Whether he was reading arguments for Darwin or arguments for Mendel, he didn't see hard proof for either theory. And he didn't think Walter Sutton had gathered enough information for his cell studies. He felt that no one had methodically shown how inheritance worked.

So, in a small lab at Columbia University, Thomas set out to figure it out himself. He gathered a group of talented students: Alfred Henry Sturtevant, Calvin Blackman Bridges, and Hermann Joseph Muller. He needed to try out his idea on a living creature with a very short life cycle,

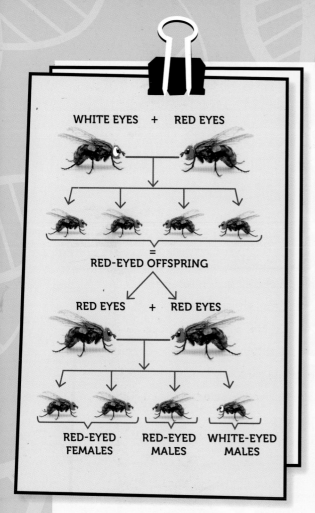

WHITE EYES + RED EYES

= RED-EYED OFFSPRING

RED EYES + RED EYES

RED-EYED FEMALES   RED-EYED MALES   WHITE-EYED MALES

so that he could study as many generations as possible in a short time. So he also gathered fruit flies. *Millions* of them. In the Fly Room, where they worked, his students got cramped desks. The flies got old milk jars and rotting bananas.

In 1910, Thomas and his students found the first random mutation in their flies: a male fly with white eyes.

Thomas's team had found an inherited trait. And they were seeing it *only in males*. The researchers knew that females—whether human or fruit fly—had two *X*-shaped chromosomes, while males had one shaped like an *X* and one shaped like a *Y*. So they guessed (correctly) that if white eyes appeared only in male flies, then the trait must be carried only on the Y chromosome.

Thomas couldn't be skeptical anymore. With more and more fly experiments, he proved to himself, and to the rest of the world, that chromosomes carried the instructions for inheritance. He even proved that certain genes along the strands of chromosomes were responsible for certain traits.

With his fruit flies and banana peels, Thomas had unlocked one of the biggest secrets of genetics. He won a Nobel Prize for his work in 1933.

GENETICS ROCK STAR

BLOODY BRILLIANT

RANDOM GENETIC MUTATIONS helped the plants and animals of Socotra adapt. Other mutations gave white eyes to male fruit flies. All very interesting, but not that useful. Did mutations ever help humans?

In 1949, a guy named J. B. S. (Jack) Haldane suggested that inheriting a disease could sometimes be useful. And that a blood disorder might actually be good for you.

Jack was an all-round genius. He started reading when he was three, worked in his father's biology lab when he was eight, and cowrote his first scientific paper at age twenty. Although he studied math and classics in school, he made major contributions to statistics, biology, physiology, and genetics. He even wrote science fiction stories!

Jack's colleagues (and even friends) thought he was a bit nuts. Why?

- He drank a hydrochloric acid solution to see what it would do to his body.

- He hyperventilated for hours to measure his symptoms.

- In World War I, he snuck behind enemy lines to set bombs.

When it came to the study of blood, Jack came up with a strange theory. He knew that many people in the Mediterranean had fewer red blood cells than normal. No one understood why. But Jack reasoned that having anemia (a lack of red blood cells) might actually protect people

Red blood cells in rush hour

from malaria—always a danger in warm, damp, climates.

Malaria had been a problem for thousands of years, so surely the human body must have had time to evolve and adapt. And some types of anemia were definitely inherited. In those cases, then, could anemia be considered a genetic mutation that gave people a better chance of surviving malaria? Jack also knew that malaria was most dangerous in kids. So, if people without adaptations were killed off young, maybe those with adaptations passed their improved genes to their offspring.

Jack made all these suggestions in the 1940s, before anyone knew with any real accuracy what DNA did. But he was right. Over the following decades, scientists proved that anemia helped combat malaria.

Fewer red blood cells means less oxygen to the body. A type of genetic anemia called sickle cell trait (SCT) can make it dangerous for people to do extreme exercise. After a study in the 1980s showed that recruits with SCT were thirty-seven times more likely to collapse in training, the US Army drew up new rules about hydration and rest breaks.

And even though anemia itself can cause health problems, the trade-off was genetically worthwhile in areas of the world where malaria was common.

Today, doctors can treat anemia, boosting a person's red blood cell count and energy levels. But thanks to Jack's theories and later research, those doctors also know that, sometimes, it's best to let the disorder go untreated.

A COLORFUL CHARACTER

IN 1990, a man named Emerson Moser retired from Crayola Crayons. He'd worked for the company for thirty-seven years, from the time when each crayon was made by hand to the time when seventy-two colors were mixed and molded by machine. He'd seen a lot of changes—but not always the same way other workers had seen them. Emerson Moser, chief crayon maker, was color-blind. Sometimes he had to check with his fellow workers to find out if he was pouring the right hue in the right place.

Like anemia, color blindness can be an inherited genetic condition. In 1986, scientists found the exact genes that control our ability—or

inability—to see the usual spectrum of colors. In Emerson Moser (or his ancestors), the DNA that makes up those genes was somehow copied a little bit differently.

Emerson lived a long and happy life despite his DNA mutation. That change in his gene occurred in a spot where the results weren't *too* serious. But what if copying errors happen in crucial places?

BEFORE HIS TIME

IN 1996, Sam Berns was born a kicking, crying, seemingly normal baby boy. But a year later, his parents were back in the doctor's office, worried about their son. He wasn't thriving. His skin seemed unusually tight, stretching over his joints.

When Sam was only twenty-two months old, doctors diagnosed a rare genetic condition called progeria—the "aging disease." It's incredibly rare. When Sam was diagnosed, there were only about a hundred known sufferers around the world. These kids aged at an accelerated rate. As toddlers, they lost their hair, and their joints became less stable. As children, they developed heart disease as if they were eighty-year-olds. There were no medicines available. There was no cure. Most

Sam with his Boston Bruins hero Zdeno Chara at Progeria Awareness Night

sufferers died when they were about thirteen years old, usually from heart attack or stroke.

Doctors broke the news: Sam would age and die at super-speed.

But Sam's parents, Scott Berns and Leslie Gordon, weren't ready to return home quietly and face that news. Scott was a pediatrician and Leslie was studying to become one. Within a couple of years, they'd created the Progeria Research Foundation, and set out to find treatments for their son and other kids like him.

In 2003, a team that included Sam's mother compared the genes of progeria sufferers with the genes of their parents. They found a mutation in a gene called LMNA, which produces proteins needed by cells. In 2009, doctors started testing the first possible medicines for the condition, using a drug that was originally developed for cancer treatment.

Sam, meanwhile, pursued his dreams. He was an avid drummer. In high school, he desperately wanted to play in the marching band. But the snare drum and harness weighed almost as much as Sam himself. He and his family hired an engineer to redesign the drum and created one that weighed only three kilograms (six pounds). Soon, Sam was marching with his bandmates.

When Sam told this and other stories at a TED conference, the video went viral. Sam Berns died on January 10, 2014, at the age of seventeen, but his video still inspires people around the world. The charity founded by his family continues to fund genetic research in hopes of giving other progeria sufferers longer, healthier lives.

DNA IN THE DEPTHS

THE WORK OF WALTER SUTTON and Thomas Hunt Morgan had proven that Gregor Mendel was right—parents passed their traits to their offspring in a generally predictable pattern. But Darwin was also right. When a random mutation helped a creature survive, that creature would pass its genes to its offspring and, eventually, those adapted offspring could take over. Finches with super-strong beaks could rule an island of the Galápagos. Trees with moisture-sucking branches could spread across the island of Socotra.

Sometimes, scientists find even more bizarre examples of creatures that have adapted to unique environments. For example:

- BROWN KIWIS To help them sniff out underground insects, these New Zealand birds have developed nostrils at the end of their beaks.

A kiwi (the bird, not the fruit)

- SUNDA PANGOLINS These anteater-like creatures from Southeast Asia dine on termites. To better slurp the insects from their mounds, they have evolved to have a super-long tongue that stretches all the way from a bone near the pelvis.

- ICEFISH These Arctic-dwelling fish absorb oxygen straight from the ocean. They don't need red blood cells to fuel their muscles.

Millions of years ago, icefish functioned like we do. Scientists know this because the fish still have a gene that—if it worked—would help build blood cells. But since the fish found a useful mutation, one that gave them a plentiful supply of direct oxygen, the blood-cell gene fell out of use. Now that unused gene is simply a remnant of the species' genetic past.

WHICH SUSPECT WILL THE DETECTIVE ELIMINATE?

HINT: Remember, this case isn't black and white— and neither were the contents of the jewelry cases.

Answer: Dr. Hacker

CODE 3 BREAKERS

YOU CAN TAKE THE RESULTS of your own genetic testing to a "portrait" company to create artwork from your personal pattern. You'll receive a glowing barcode of colored stripes to hang on your wall. You can even choose the color palette, the size, and the frame.

Obviously, our ability to visualize DNA has come a long way. Just a hundred years ago, scientists had no idea what it looked like. They knew it lived in the center of cells. They knew it controlled heredity. But they didn't know its size, shape, or form. DNA was simply too small to see under the microscopes available at that time.

Then came the field of X-ray crystallography. We usually think of X-rays as tools for diagnosing broken bones. But X-rays are actually a lot like light. Just as you can bounce light off a mirror, researchers learned to bounce and scatter X-rays off crystals. Then they used the pattern made by the bouncing rays to trace the shape of the crystal. When scientists want to study the shape of a particular molecule, they take a sample of the molecules in a solution, mix it with a special liquid to form tiny droplets, and then let the liquid evaporate. At that point, the solution becomes more concentrated and a three-dimensional crystal pattern forms. Not all molecules easily take crystal form but, luckily for the researchers, DNA molecules do!

Figuring out the form of a molecule through X-ray crystallography is like looking at a bunch of overlapping reflections—a bit tricky, in other words. It would take several expert X-ray bouncers to decode the images of DNA crystals and create pictures of the genetic code for the very first time. Then it would take several more scientists to turn those images into a model that everyone could see and understand.

GENETICS ROCK STAR

X-RAY EXPERT

AS A LITTLE GIRL IN THE 1930s, Rosalind Franklin attended St. Paul's Girls' School in London, England, one of the only schools in the city that taught science to girls. Rosalind learned the basics of biology and chemistry while still in elementary school.

And that was lucky, because Rosalind's love of science grew and grew. She'd grow up to become one of the most important researchers in the field of genetics.

After she earned her PhD at Cambridge University, she moved to Paris. There she became an expert in X-ray crystallography. Mostly, she made pictures of viruses. She gained renown in her field, publishing almost fifty papers and speaking at events around the world. When she started making pictures of DNA too, she shared those images with another researcher, named Maurice Wilkins.

Rosalind wasn't the first person to create an image of DNA through X-ray crystallography. But earlier images were so blurry and confusing, scientists couldn't quite figure out what they were looking at. Many tried to make models of shapes that would explain all those reflections and shadows, but none of the models made sense.

Rosalind's pictures were different. She showed that there were two different forms of DNA crystals, which she called the A form and the B form. In early images, those forms were mixed, but Rosalind had managed to capture one form at a time. In her images, DNA appeared more clearly than ever before. She could see that:

- Each strand had two "backbones" with chemicals attached.
- One backbone and its chemicals held a pattern that started at the top and went down.
- The other backbone's pattern started at the bottom and went up.

She'd discovered that the two DNA backbones were like mirror images of each other—a discovery that changed the way scientists thought about the code, and about the structure of the molecule itself.

Then, tragically, Rosalind died of cancer. She was only thirty-seven years old. Her tombstone reads: "Her work on viruses was of lasting bene-fit to mankind." Which was true. But in 1958, no one yet recognized what an amazing thing Rosalind had begun by creating images of DNA. In fact, most people still didn't know that DNA existed. So no one predicted that while Rosalind's work on viruses would be mostly forgotten, her work on DNA would become famous around the world.

SPLITTING STRANDS

ROSALIND CAPTURED HER IMAGES of DNA as it was stretched thin, the way it might be just before it was replicated inside a cell. Every second, your body makes millions of new cells. It does this by dividing its existing cells. Inside each cell, the information is carefully copied. Then—*pop!* The cell splits itself into two.

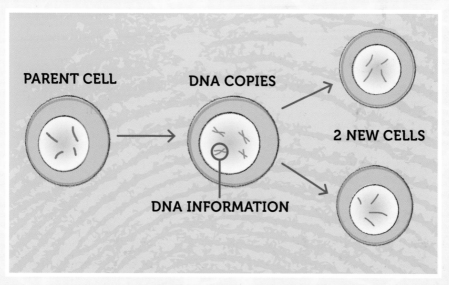

PARENT CELL

DNA COPIES

2 NEW CELLS

DNA INFORMATION

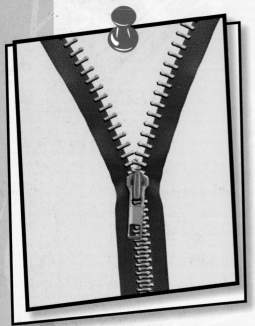

But copying DNA is a tricky thing. Before a cell divides, 3 billion units of code must be reproduced.

Fortunately, there are microscopic "factory workers" called enzymes to do the grunt work inside each cell. First, they detach the two DNA backbones, separating them the way you might separate the two sides of a zipper. Then they begin to meticulously copy.

Attached to each strand of DNA are the four bases: A, T, C, and G (adenine, thymine, cytosine, guanine). An A always connects to a T, and a C always connects to a G. The enzymes set to work creating the correct base to match each unit of code. When they reach an A, they build a T. When they see a C, they build a G. And when they're finished, they've created a mirror image of each backbone. There are now two strands of DNA. Each strand has one "mother" side and a new "daughter" side. Once the DNA is copied, the cell can divide. One cell has become two, each with its matching DNA.

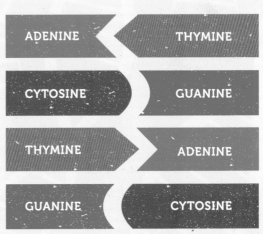

GENETICS ROCK STAR

SHUTTER BUGS

WHILE ROSALIND SPENT her childhood studying science, Maurice Wilkins spent his youth building instruments. He loved microscopes and telescopes, and even made his own lenses. As an adult, Maurice put these skills to use as the head of a biophysics unit at King's College in London, England. He designed his own equipment for separating tiny DNA fibers, and his own cameras for photographing them. Like Rosalind, he was an expert in X-ray crystallography. And like Rosalind, he captured increasingly clear images.

He was convinced that DNA was shaped like a spiral. If he took enough X-rays, he was sure he could prove it.

In 1950, Maurice took his best images to a conference, where he showed them to an enthusiastic young scientist named James Watson. When Rosalind sent Maurice a particularly great DNA image that she'd captured, Maurice passed that one along too.

He was sharing the best collection of DNA images ever produced.

A MAN, A PLAN, A CANAL —PANAMA!

PALINDROMES read the same forward or backward. They can be single words, such as *mom* and *dad*. Or they can be longer phrases, such as *never odd or even*.

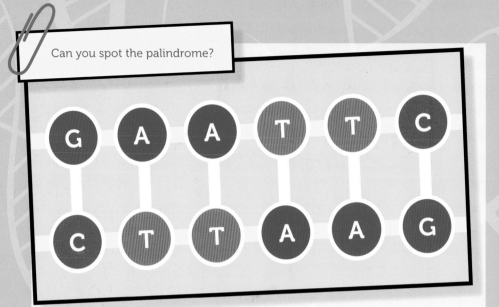

Palindromes don't exist only in English. They've been found in ancient Roman, Hebrew, and Sanskrit texts. They're popular in poetry in many parts of the world, and in pop culture. There are even Pokémon characters with palindrome names.

As researchers learned more about DNA, they could see that the long strands—the railings of the spiral staircase—were joined by the chemical bases called A, G, C, and T. And as they looked more closely, they could see that those bases were arranged in patterns. For example, one section might read G-A-A-T-T-C, while a mirrored piece might read C-T-T-A-A-G.

Scientists realized they were seeing a code within the human body, and much of that code was written in palindromes.

Some people see art as well as science in the palindrome patterns of DNA. Religious leaders often point to the perfect microscopic spirals and repeating poem-like codes within our cells as evidence a supreme being created life on earth.

GENETICS ROCK STAR

A PERSISTENT PAIRING

AMERICAN RESEARCHER JAMES WATSON had two degrees in biology by the time he was twenty-three years old. He took a job at Cambridge University in London in 1951, then traveled to a conference in Italy, where he saw Maurice Wilkins's images of DNA.

He was fascinated.

He rushed back to Cambridge and convinced a man named Francis Crick to help him create a model showing exactly what DNA looked like. Francis was supposed to be studying X-ray crystallography and blood cells, but James was persuasive. Soon, the two were immersed in the latest DNA research. They gathered bits of information from scientists all over the world. It was like trying to build a thousand-piece puzzle when different scientists had different puzzle pieces—and a few pieces were missing altogether. Many people—including Maurice Wilkins—told them they were crazy to try.

But James and Francis were determined. They collected all the pieces they could:

- Thanks to Rosalind Franklin and Maurice Wilkins, they had images of DNA crystals.

- After meeting an Austrian-American biochemist

named Erwin Chargaff, they learned one of "Chargaff's rules": There were equal numbers of A and T bases in DNA, and equal numbers of G and C.

- American chemist and activist Linus Pauling (who later won a Nobel Prize in Chemistry *and* a Nobel Peace Prize) had shown that some protein molecules in blood cells were shaped like helixes, or spirals.

Taking all this information and more, James and Francis set out to create a model of what DNA looked like. They came up with an initial version and eagerly invited their fellow scientists to view it. Rosalind saw it and scoffed. It would never stick together if it were formed like that, she said. In fact, reactions to their draft model were so terrible that the college asked James and Francis to please stop building examples until more information was found.

But they didn't. They kept researching and thinking and building until they arrived at what they were *sure* was the true shape of DNA. Their final model was a double helix (a spiral-staircase shape). They showed the way the two long strands could stretch and split to be copied, then rejoin into a spiral once again. And they showed that the ladder rungs inside the staircase were units of code.

Francis felt that he and James were on the brink of something amazing.

Francis went home one day and told his wife he'd made a huge, world-changing discovery. She just nodded and smiled. Apparently, he said things like that all the time.

SHAPE SHIFTING

IMAGINE BUILDING the most complicated house of cards the world has ever seen, then asking your best friend to make an exact copy of it. Except instead of giving your friend your house to look at, you give him photographs of its shadows.

That's sort of what James and Francis had to do—make a model of one of the most complicated shapes in the universe, using pictures of the shape's scattered X-rays. They built their model with an array of brass rods and balls and a collection of ring stands from their labs—thin metal stands with clamps attached. When it was finished, the whole thing looked like a giant construction of Tinkertoys.

Time magazine sent a young photographer named Antony Barrington Brown to take a picture of the two scientists with their finished model. Antony had no idea what DNA was, and no idea what their discovery meant. But he told the men to stand in front of their model and look important. He snapped the shot.

Although Antony was paid for his photo, it wasn't used for a long time. Then, all of sudden, the world realized what a massive discovery James and Francis had really made. They'd created an image of the building blocks of human life. They were famous. And so was Antony's photo.

James (left) and Francis (right) showing off their model marvel

GAIN AND GLORY

WHILE JAMES AND FRANCIS were busy building models, Rosalind Franklin also had figured out the true shape of DNA. She wrote two papers explaining the spiral-staircase idea. At least one of these was written before she saw the model made by James and Francis, and the three of them were all published in the same scientific journal at the same time.

So, who discovered the true shape of DNA? Well, James and Francis would never have figured it out without the images produced by Rosalind and Maurice. But other people wouldn't have understood it nearly as well without the model made by James and Francis.

In 1962, James, Francis, and Maurice earned a Nobel Prize for discovering the structure of DNA. Unfortunately, Rosalind Franklin had no share in the glory—she'd died four years before, and only living people can receive the Nobel Prize.

THE SUSPECTS ALL VOLUNTEERED DNA SAMPLES. I GUESS WITHHOLDING WOULD HAVE MADE THEM LOOK GUILTY.

ARE WE STILL WAITING FOR LAB RESULTS?

YUP, WE HAD ONE PERSON'S DNA INFO ALREADY, THOUGH, AND IT WASN'T A MATCH. GUESS WE CAN RULE OUT ANOTHER SUSPECT.

WHICH SUSPECT DID NOT HAVE TO BE ASKED FOR A DNA SAMPLE?

DEE ZASTER
CASHIER

RUSTY HAMMER
CASHIER

TERRY BILL
CONVICTED THIEF

CAMMIE SOLE
STORE MANAGER

ELLA VADER
LOCAL SECURITY GUARD

STAN STILL
SALES REPRESENTATIVE

DAISY PICKER
OWNS THE STORE NEXT DOOR

DWAYNE PIPE
CUSTODIAN

PIA NUTT
SUPERMODEL,
REGULAR CUSTOMER

HAZEL NUTT
SUPERMODEL,
REGULAR CUSTOMER

IDA GOTTAWAY
STORE BOOKKEEPER

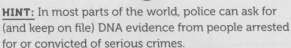

HINT: In most parts of the world, police can ask for (and keep on file) DNA evidence from people arrested for or convicted of serious crimes.

Answer: Terry Bill

HOT ON THE TRAIL

AHOY, MATEY! What's say you and me make ourselves a treasure map? We be lookin' for a gene to cure all the ills of humanity, and *X* marks the spot!

Well, maybe the geneticists didn't talk like pirates. But they *did* set out to make a treasure map. In the 1980s, a team of scientists decided to map all the genes in human DNA. Together, the genes in the human body are known as the "genome," so the researchers called their quest the Human Genome Project.

Not all the bits of code in our DNA form genes. Much of that code is instructions for turning genes on and off, or it's extra, unused material. The genes themselves are pieces of DNA

associated with inherited traits. Remember the ladder shape of DNA, with rungs between the strands? Our genes are groups of ladder rungs.

As they embarked on the Human Genome Project, scientists hoped to catalog our genes and create a sort of treasure map for doctors and researchers all over the world. Need to identify the genes responsible for sight? Here's where to look. Want to test treatments for diabetes? Here's the gene associated with diabetes. The project would reveal so much genetic information, and share it with so many labs around the world, that many speculated it would soon end disease, starvation, and suffering.

At least, that's what they imagined.

But there were problems deciding who would do the research, who would get the credit, and who would be allowed to make money from the results. And then there were the results themselves.

The human genome itself turned out to be much more complicated than anyone had expected.

FLY TRACKS

BACK IN THE FLY ROOM in 1911, one of Thomas Hunt Morgan's students, Alfred Sturtevant, tracked a mutated gene as it was passed from generation to generation of fruit flies. To make it easier to find and track

This is a simplified version of Alfred's gene map. The chromosome is represented by the long white bar. The vertical colored bars show the locations of the mutated genes.

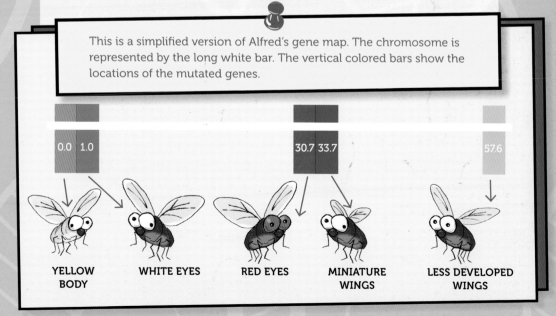

| 0.0 | 1.0 | | 30.7 | 33.7 | | 57.6 |

| YELLOW BODY | WHITE EYES | RED EYES | MINIATURE WINGS | LESS DEVELOPED WINGS |

the mutation, Alfred created a diagram. It showed how the gene was constructed (which of the four chemical bases appeared, in what order) and where it occurred along the DNA strand.

This was the very first DNA map.

But Alfred tracked only one gene. To track more, and figure out the order in which they appeared, would take a mastermind of patterns.

GENETICS ROCK STAR

PROTEIN POWER

ONE NOBEL PRIZE wasn't enough for Frederick Sanger: this overachiever won two.

He earned his first for his discoveries about insulin, the hormone that helps our bodies regulate sugar and fat. Until Frederick's research, scientists thought the proteins in insulin were just little clouds of material that floated around, in no particular order. Frederick proved otherwise. He found a distinct pattern within the proteins, like a fingerprint.

That may seem like a tiny detail, but it was an important one. The idea that proteins formed patterns won Frederick the Nobel Prize in Chemistry in 1958. In turn, this research helped Francis Crick (the guy working on DNA models) to discover that the ladder rungs in DNA were also distributed in meaningful patterns—codes that instructed the body to make certain shapes of proteins. Without Frederick's work, James Watson and Francis Crick couldn't have built their DNA model.

But Frederick wasn't finished. In the 1970s, he worked with another scientist, Alan Coulson, to take X-ray pictures of DNA and record the patterns along an individual strand. They examined the "ladder rungs" in the DNA of a bacterium and recorded its sequence of 5,386 bases. In 1977, Frederick found an even faster way of recording the patterns—that was the discovery that earned him his second Nobel Prize in Chemistry.

SEQUENCING SCRAMBLE

IF ALFRED COULD TRACE a fruit fly gene, and Frederick could track DNA patterns, then the world's best scientists should be able to map the entire human genome, right? That was the theory behind the Human Genome Project.

The U.S. government provided funding to an organization called the National Center for Human Genome Research so it could start the

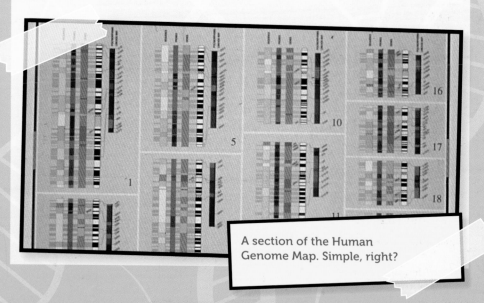

A section of the Human Genome Map. Simple, right?

work. The project also drew top genetics researchers from around the world. Since no one team could do the huge job alone, labs from Britain, Japan, France, Germany, and China signed on to contribute. Some worked on new research methods to make the mapping process faster. Others worked on individual genes.

But in 1998, a group called the Celera Corporation realized that if it could use faster sequencing techniques, it might be able to decode the human genome first, before the government-funded labs of the world. And that might give the corporation some major advantages.

A private company would have the option to hold on to whatever information it gathered while considering how to profit from it—unlike the government-funded labs, which released their information to the public every day. Other scientists would still get access to the information fairly quickly. But if a company could catalog all the human genes, maybe it could charge scientists to search the catalog. Or, if it was first to identify certain disease-inducing genes, maybe it could develop, produce, and sell the drugs to treat genetic diseases.

Some people liked the idea. Corporate research was almost always faster than government research. Maybe getting drug companies involved would mean quicker, better treatments for genetic diseases.

But as news of Celera Corporation's plans spread, other people began to worry. If private companies were allowed to claim specific research rights, or withhold genetic information from the public, would that lead to corporations *owning* human genes?

ETHICAL DILEMMAS

IF A CORPORATION INVESTS the time and money to invent a machine or create a medicine, that corporation owns the result. It gets a patent, a sort of international claim certificate, which means no one else can steal its ideas. The corporation then has the exclusive right to sell its machine or drug and make a profit.

So, if a corporation invests a lot of time and money to investigate a gene, instead of a machine, shouldn't it still get a patent? Shouldn't it be the only one allowed to develop medicines or treatments based on that gene, so it can make its money back?

If thousands of corporations helped to figure out what genes do, that would benefit people everywhere. But without patents, and the chance to make money on treatments, there would be no motivation for corporations to decode genes. Discovery should equal ownership.

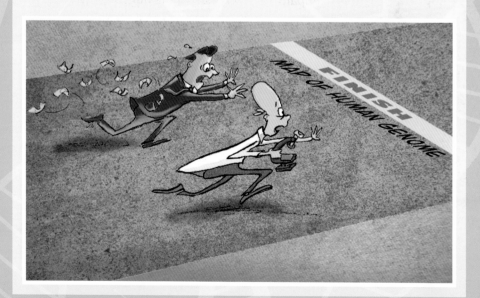

Those were the arguments of people who believed private companies would do the best job of gene research.

The scientists of the Human Genome Project thought differently. They believed that gene research should be available free to everyone— free to researchers working in tiny, underfunded labs, and free to major corporations doing drug research.

These scientists grew so concerned that a private company might claim ownership of genes that they sped up the entire Human Genome Project. Then they sped it up again. They spurred developments in computer technology so the mapping would go faster. And with each increase in efficiency, they posted more and more information online. All for free. In 2000, researchers revealed a draft map of the entire genome.

By 2001, the international research group and Celera were basically tied. There would be no clear winner in the Human Genome Race. They called a truce and jointly released a working draft (like a rough copy) of their research. And in 2003, the international researchers declared their map of the genome complete. Thanks to their speedy work, scientists around the world could freely download the human genome. Celera, meanwhile, began researching personalized medicine—tests and treatments designed specifically to suit a patient's unique genetic code.

Companies continued to claim individual genes for research. But in June 2013, the U.S. Supreme Court declared that DNA in its natural form can't be patented. Other courts around the world are still debating the issue, but most seem to be following the U.S. lead.

So you're in luck: the genes within your body belong entirely to you. Private companies can research human genes and create medicines to affect them, but they can't *own* parts of your DNA.

Opponents of gene patents say that DNA is the basis of life, and life is not a product to be bought or sold.

THE DATING POOL

IF TWO PEOPLE with different gene mutations have a baby, that baby will likely not inherit either of those mutations. The child will inherit genes from its mother to balance the gene mutations of its father, and vice versa. It's part of the body's double-checking process. We have extra copies of our DNA instructions to help make sure we're born healthy.

Unless . . . our parents have identical mutations.

Closely related parents might both carry recessive genes for the same ailments and deformities, and increase the likelihood of passing them on. This can happen in isolated places where populations are small and families intermarry often. Places like the fishing outposts of Newfoundland. There, a high number of people suffer from a rare heart condition. Doctors diagnosed a problem with the pumping of the right ventricle, but they didn't know how to cure it, or how to diagnose it in advance. Sometimes, there were no symptoms until a patient dropped dead. And that happened fairly often—50 percent of men with the disease and 5 percent of women died before they reached the age of forty.

Eventually, doctors figured out how to implant a tiny machine beside the heart. If someone's heartbeats grew too irregular, or stopped, the machine would shock the heart back into action. But for the machine to be useful, doctors needed to know which Newfoundland residents were at risk.

That's where genetic researchers came in.

In 2007, thanks to the Human Genome Project, they found the gene mutation responsible for the problem. Then they set out to find families who carried the gene. Today, members of those families can have their genes tested long before they experience any heart symptoms. That way, doctors can implant the heart-shocking machine for the people who need it.

For Newfoundland residents, the Human Genome Project and the medical research that came after it meant that fewer people died young, and more families lived long lives together.

THE ICELAND APP

IT'S A CRISP, MOONLIT NIGHT. When Ari and Anna lock eyes at a party, it's love at first sight. They share a romantic kiss on the streets of Reykjavík.

The next day, Ari heads off to his family reunion, eager to tell his parents about the new love of his life. But wait . . . what's Anna doing at his party?

She's his second cousin?!?

Gross!

Does this scene sound unlikely? Well, things like this happen more than you'd think in Iceland. The island nation has only 326,000 people, most from families who've lived there for countless generations. That means many people in Iceland have tons of cousins. So many cousins, they can't keep track of them all.

People don't want to accidentally date their relatives. And genetically, it's a bad idea. Cousins are more likely to have genes with the same mutations, and their kids can inherit genetic problems.

Smartphones to the rescue.

Three University of Iceland engineering students designed an app. Now when two people bump their phones together, the app analyzes their family trees and tells them whether or not they're cousins—*before* they start dating.

There are plenty of fish in the Icelandic sea. And now everyone knows which fish are safe to date.

CLUB REYKJAVIK

MORE PRELIMINARY RESULTS FROM THE LAB. FIRST OF ALL, THE SUSPECT HAS TWO X CHROMOSOMES.

GREAT. THAT TAKES FOUR MALES OFF THE LIST.

THERE'S MORE. THE TESTS SHOW GENETIC HERITAGE. THE SUSPECT HAS 100 PERCENT SCANDINAVIAN ANCESTRY.

HMM ... PEOPLE IN SCANDINAVIA EVOLVED SEPARATELY FROM THOSE IN THE REST OF EUROPE. ISOLATED BY OCEAN AND MOUNTAINS. I KNOW WHAT THAT MEANS.

WHO CAN YOU REMOVE FROM THE SUSPECT LIST?

DEE ZASTER
CASHIER

RUSTY HAMMER
CASHIER

IPA GOTTAWAY
STORE BOOKKEEPER

CAMMIE SOLE
STORE MANAGER

ELLA VADER
LOCAL SECURITY GUARD

STAN STILL
SALES REPRESENTATIVE

DAISY PICKER
OWNS THE STORE NEXT DOOR

DWAYNE PIPE
CUSTODIAN

PIA NUTT
SUPERMODEL,
REGULAR CUSTOMER

HAZEL NUTT
SUPERMODEL,
REGULAR CUSTOMER

HINT: If the criminal has two X chromosomes and Scandinavian ancestry, *she* probably has classic northern European coloring: fair skin and blonde hair.

Answer: Dee Zaster, Rusty Hammer, Ida Gottaway, Stan Still, Daisy Picker, and Dwayne Pipe

RED HERRINGS 5

WHEN GREGOR MENDEL CROSSED pea plant varieties in the 1800s, he was experimenting with DNA. He was taking genes from one variety of pea plant and giving them to another. He just didn't know it. He could see the end results, but not the genes involved.

Modern geneticists have a lot more science at their fingertips. They can identify individual genes and transfer them between plants to create new, specially designed products. This has led to an array of genetically modified organisms, from the corn in your breakfast cereal to the soybeans in your stir-fry sauce. (There are even genetically modified pets on the market!)

Researchers are also learning more about DNA copies and clones. They're exploring the genetic similarities and differences between twins to see which of our human characteristics are caused by genes, and which by our environments. They're even making their own multiples. Labs can now clone mice, pigs, and sheep so scientists can do research on animals with identical DNA.

WHO'S YOUR STYLIST?

Scientists have removed a hair-growth gene from the mouse on the left.

Soon, scientists may be able to do things that once seemed impossible: cure spinal cord injuries, save endangered species, and bring extinct creatures back to life. Only one thing's for sure: in his pea-plant garden of 1865, Gregor could never have dreamed of the possibilities humans are exploring today.

EARTHY EXPERIMENTS

MONSANTO, AN AMERICAN-OWNED multinational chemical company, was the first to genetically modify a plant cell, in 1982. The company was exploring a field called "biotechnology": combining biology and technology to revolutionize farming. By 1996, Monsanto had released three new products:

- cotton seeds with built-in protection against insects;
- soybeans that thrived while herbicides killed surrounding weeds;
- a hormone to make dairy cows produce more milk.

Other companies quickly followed Monsanto's lead. Together, they made plenty of arguments in favor of genetically modified organisms (GMOs):

- GMOs produce more food, faster. They can feed the hungry around the world.
- GMOs resist pests, so farmers can use less poison.
- GMOs can be engineered to need less water, so droughts won't cause crop failures.

The perfect milk machine?

For some people, genetically modified plants might prove to be life-changing. Imagine you've suffered for years from diabetes. Then one day you see your doctor and get this prescription: Lettuce.

It just might happen.

Professor Henry Daniell in Florida has spent years developing a kind of lettuce that provides insulin. Instead of relying on daily injections, people with diabetes might one day munch a few lettuce leaves and receive enough insulin to keep their bodies running smoothly. The leaves could even be dried and packaged.

Not only is this easier than traditional treatments, it's much cheaper. In some developing countries, the cost of diabetes medicine is half of what the average person earns. So far, studies on insulin lettuce have been done on mice, not people. But if the treatment for diabetes becomes lettuce leaves instead of costly medicine, thousands of lives could be saved.

NOT SO FAST

GMO-FREE!

Non-GMO Verified!

Have you ever seen those lines on food packages? If GMOs are fast-growing, insect-repelling, and safe, why doesn't everyone want to eat them?

Well, there are plenty of people who think scientists have gone overboard with their plant genetics. Organic farmers and health activists say people should be eating pure, natural food, not genetically modified crops. They say no one knows for sure whether GMOs are safe.

Why not? For one thing, genes are usually responsible for more than one function in an organism. Some people fear that when scientists take

It's "Just Say No to GMO" at this protest march.

genes from one plant and stick them in another, they may get more than they expect. What if a toxin is accidentally introduced, causing cancer in humans a decade from now? What if viruses learn from the supposedly virus-proof plants and mutate into new diseases? What if modifications cause new allergic reactions?

If you're a North American kid, you've likely eaten a genetically modified plant today. Was there any corn in your breakfast cereal? Did that muffin at recess contain soybean or canola oil? Almost all of the corn, soybeans, and canola grown in North America are genetically modified. Health Canada and the U.S. Food and Drug Administration maintain that the products are safe.

But in Europe, governments have decided that the public's health concerns are valid. Or, at least, that the questions haven't all been answered yet. The laws of the European Union say that every single GMO product has to be thoroughly tested and approved by food-safety scientists. So far, those scientists have said okay to some animal feed. Human food has gotten a big "no, thanks." And only one genetically modified crop—a kind of corn—can be planted there.

GMOs are so new and so controversial that different laws are constantly being considered, and countries are choosing a wide range of regulations. It seems as if only time will tell who's right.

SEED WARS

ORDER IN THE COURT! On one side of the case is Farmer Joe. He's planted canola, wheat, and corn on his farm for decades, and he's committed to raising only the purest, most natural crops. On the other side of the case is Biotech Giant. It sold its genetically modified seeds to the farmers east and west of Farmer Joe's fields.

PROBLEM NUMBER ONE: Pollen from the genetically modified crops is blowing into Farmer Joe's fields. It's getting mixed up with his plants. Now they're not pure, organic, nonmodified crops. And unless he can somehow stop the wind from blowing, he can't prevent it from happening every single season.

PROBLEM NUMBER TWO: Biotech Giant has patented its GMO products. It *owns* that blowing pollen. And if its crops are now growing in Farmer Joe's field, it doesn't matter whether the wind blew the pollen or he planted genetically modified seeds himself. He's growing Biotech products, so he should have to pay Biotech for the rights.

Or should he?

Cases just like this one are making their way through North American courts. And just as soon as one court announces Farmer Joe is right, another court overturns the decision. In some cases, biotech companies have simply promised not to sue individual farmers, and the courts have accepted that compromise. But organic farmers say that's not good enough—it doesn't stop GMO pollen from blowing onto their organic fields.

If you were the judge, what would you decide?

BANKING ON GENETICS

DNA IS THE BASIC building block of life. Its spirals held the instructions for Gregor Mendel's pea plants, Walter Sutton's grasshoppers, and Thomas Hunt Morgan's fruit flies. But what if species are threatened, like the dragon's blood tree of Socotra? Their DNA—their secret codes of life—could disappear from the earth forever.

Like the dragon's blood tree, many plants are threatened by climate change. Others, from strangely colored tomato varieties to less productive wheat hybrids, are phased out as farmers switch to better-growing crops. And scientists worry that still other plants could be wiped out by diseases or natural disasters.

To ensure the world doesn't lose precious DNA diversity, researchers have founded various seed banks. These are like warehouses that can store seeds for hundreds of years. Some are dedicated to preserving seeds for food crops; others, for endangered plants. Still others are working to catalog and store as many seeds as possible from all over the world.

On an icebound island halfway between Norway and the North

Pole, the Svalbard Global Seed Vault stores its samples inside a mountain. There, seeds are buried deep within layers of rock, protected by permafrost. Even if an asteroid struck the earth, even if we all lost electrical power, the seeds within the seed vault would survive.

It's an international safe-deposit box for DNA.

ANIMAL CROSSING

LOOKING FOR A NEW PET? How about a nice glow-in-the-dark fish? It's a regular zebrafish with some extra light-reflecting cells, courtesy of a genetics lab. When it was offered for sale in the United States in 2003, it became the first genetically modified pet on the market.

These incandescent swimmers didn't start out as novelty items. Professors in Singapore and Taiwan developed the fish to help detect water pollution. When tiny amounts of pollutants were present in lakes or streams, the fish would glow.

Pet companies quickly saw the appeal of the unique creatures. After all, the pet market in Asia was booming. And people in North America already spent billions of dollars each year on fish food and cat collars, fancy doggie day cares and hamster jackets. If stores could offer unique hybrids, they might attract adventurous buyers.

Chicago artist Eduardo Kac once added genes from Pacific Northwest jellyfish to the DNA of a rabbit. Voilà! A luminescent bunny. Animal-rights activists went wild, claiming that Eduardo was playing with the basis of life, pretending to be God. But Eduardo wasn't commenting about whether the genetic modification of animals was good or bad. And scientists had already been experimenting with these technologies for some time. Eduardo simply drew an imaginary frame around the issue and presented it as art, to draw the public's attention to it. As an artist who had previously hooked himself intravenously to a robot (to symbolize the relationships between humans and technology) and implanted a tracking chip in his leg (to raise questions about privacy and security), Eduardo was used to stirring up controversy.

His work raised interesting questions, the same questions that many scientists, academics, animal-rights activists, ethicists, and even potential pet buyers are asking: Just how far can scientists go with crossed species and mixed-up DNA? Is it ethical to juggle with another creature's genes? Or with our own?

Genetically modified pets: a fishy business?

Some animal-rights activists argue that pets should never be genetically altered. They say that genetically modifying animals in the lab is treating animals like products.

But not everyone agrees. Pet shoppers in Asia and the United States have now bought hundreds of millions of glowing fish. Apparently, they have no concerns about genetically modified pets—at least not the fishy variety.

DOUBLE TROUBLE

DO YOU KNOW ANY IDENTICAL TWINS? Can you tell them apart?

Every once in a while, after a father's sperm has fertilized a mother's egg, the resulting cell divides in two. These matching cells grow into matching fetuses and—once in every thousand births around the world—identical twins emerge.

Until fairly recently, it was believed that identical twins had identical DNA—after all, identical twins start as one fertilized egg, with one set of DNA coding. But it turns out that's not quite true. As the twins develop, long before birth, some rare DNA mutations can occur—not many, but because cells are reproducing trillions of times, a very few small differences can happen. And the environment can play a role too, before and after the twins are born, causing small but significant changes when it comes to which of their genes are working and which are inactive.

How do we know for sure that identical twins are not completely identical? They have different fingerprints!

Twins fascinate geneticists. Studying human beings is a tricky business. Usually, it's difficult to tell which traits come from DNA and which come from environment. Is it nature or nurture? For example, your

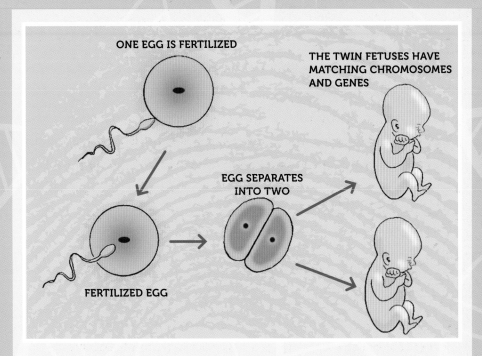

ONE EGG IS FERTILIZED

THE TWIN FETUSES HAVE MATCHING CHROMOSOMES AND GENES

EGG SEPARATES INTO TWO

FERTILIZED EGG

next-door neighbor might have a hot temper. Is that because he was born that way? Or did he have a rough childhood and develop a temper to help him cope?

Experiments with twins help scientists answer these questions. If your angry next-door neighbor has a twin brother, and that brother is calm, soft-spoken, and patient, then you can conclude that anger is not genetic. Something must have happened to your neighbor to change his personality—not his DNA.

One of the first doctors to use a "twin study" was a German skin-disease expert named Hermann Werner Siemens. In 1924, Hermann counted the number of moles on twins. He found that mole counts in identical twins were twice as similar as mole counts in fraternal twins (who share only half their DNA). He proved that moles were at least partly genetic.

No one cared too much about Hermann's moles. But researchers all over the world saw the value in his twin study. Since Hermann's time, scientists have used twins to study stress hormones, teenage smoking, lung capacity, ear deformities, eyesight, and everything in between.

By comparing twins who grew up together with twins who were adopted and grew up in different families, scientists can even study which personality traits people are born with, and which ones come from our home lives. For example, Dutch twin studies show that a love for adventure sports, like skydiving, say, is caused half by genetics and half by upbringing. Religious beliefs aren't genetic at all—those come almost entirely from family. But people who smoke are influenced by a combination of genetics, family situations, and wider environments.

Twins have been used in thousands of studies around the world. In fact, the only thing more useful than twins in scientific research is triplets. Or quadruplets. Or—wait!—what about thousands and thousands of clones?

GENETICS ROCK STAR

DOLLY THE SHEEP

CLONES ARE EXACT COPIES. Like twins, they begin as matching cells and grow into matching organisms. And that's useful for scientists because they know that all clones have exactly the same DNA. If one organism turns out differently, the reason can't be genetic.

The idea of cloning drew international attention in 1996 with the birth of Dolly the Sheep.

HOW TO CLONE A SHEEP:

- Take a normal egg cell from a sheep and scoop out its nucleus.

- Take a cell from another sheep (in Dolly's case, this egg was from a sheep's udder) and inject it into the egg cell, so that the new, combined cell has this sheep's DNA.

- Give the newly combined cell a tiny electric shock, to start it copying and dividing.

- Implant that cell into the womb of a female sheep, and watch the pregnancy progress.

This is what Ian Wilmut and his fellow Edinburgh scientists did. Dolly the Sheep was born healthy and identical to the donor of the implanted nucleus.

It had taken Ian and his crew 276 tries, but they had successfully copied their first mammal. They'd created an animal that had DNA completely identical to the DNA of the donor. With this technology, laboratories went on to produce identical copies of mice, cows, monkeys, and pigs.

An embryo is a group of cells in the very earliest stages of development. You were an embryo inside your mother's womb for the first eight weeks of her pregnancy. After that, you became a fetus.

COPIES AND CLONES

NO ONE NEEDS TO COUNT the moles or test the effects of smoking on animals. So why would anyone want identical sheep? Well, it's not about the wool. Scientists can test medicines on cloned animals and know that varying DNA doesn't affect their experiments. They can learn about animal behavior, and whether it comes from nature or nurture. But researchers in favor of cloning research say the possibilities go even further. Here are just a few of the things they hope to one day do:

- Clone human organs, so people don't have to wait on transplant lists.

- Clone cells that don't naturally regenerate, such as nerve cells, to help people recover from spinal cord injuries.

- Make healthy heart cells, then inject them into damaged hearts.

- Copy the cells of parents, so couples who can't have children naturally can have their own (genetically identical) kids.

Could genetically modified humans adapt better to space travel? Some researchers suggest that if we alter our bones for lower gravity, change our sleep rhythms to suit longer days, and strengthen our skin to resist radiation, we could survive the long journey and even adapt to life on planet Mars.

Some of these things are already underway. In 2013, scientists in Japan applied for permission to begin growing human organs inside pigs. They proposed combining human cells with pig embryos. When implanted in a pig's womb, the embryo would grow. And once the piglet was born (with a human organ inside), the organ could be removed, then transplanted into a person in need. The scientists had already successfully tried the procedure using rats and mice.

Opponents of cloning say the technology is going too far, too quickly. They say that even by cloning research animals, scientists are creating living creatures just to experiment on them and then destroy them. They also wonder what will happen if scientists start cloning human cells. Would cloned babies be used in laboratories?

Fortunately, there's no need to worry about that issue just yet—the cloning of humans has been banned by governments around the world. Even cloning human organs, as the Japanese research team proposed, hasn't yet gained support.

ON THE BRINK

IN BORNEO, palm oil is big business. To produce enough oil to feed the world's processed-food industries, loggers have hacked away the rainforest and created palm plantations.

This is great for potato chip addicts, but not such a good plan for Sumatran rhinos. They've lost their habitat. The few dozen that remain are mercilessly hunted for their horns, which are sold as medicine on the black market.

Frantic to save the animals, conservationists are trying to round up survivors, hoping they can be bred in captivity. At the Cincinnati Zoo, a rare pair has successfully produced three calves. And back in Borneo, scientists are trying to help other females conceive.

They may not be successful. There are so few animals left, and so many are injured, that it might prove impossible to save the species this way. And the rhino calves that are produced by this small parent group may be too genetically similar to build a stable population. Plus, the rhino's rainforest homes aren't growing back any time soon. Even if scientists manage to create rhino families, will they ever again roam free?

Scientists don't have all the answers, but they do have a wild backup plan. At a lab in Borneo, tissue samples from several rhinos have been carefully frozen. It's just barely possible that if geneticists learn more about cloning over the coming decades, they might be able to defrost the samples, clone the DNA, and—most difficult of all—grow new baby rhinos to term.

It's a long shot.

Restarting a species with a small selection of animals doesn't provide that important genetic diversity. And although researchers managed to clone Dolly the Sheep, experiments on endangered animals have been less successful. In 2000, a lab in Massachusetts gathered samples from a male gaur, or Indian bison, native to Southeast Asia. They attempted to clone the animal. They implanted 692 nucleuses into healthy egg cells. Eighty-one of those began to divide and

develop. Forty-two managed to grow into embryos and were implanted in female cows. Eight cows became pregnant. Only one delivered a healthy baby gaur.

Little Noah, the gaur, was the first successfully cloned endangered animal. Unfortunately, he died from an infection two days after his birth.

While results are slowly improving, cloning at-risk species is still a complicated and expensive process. Many conservationists say it would be better to use the money and energy to preserve habitat. Or to save creatures with better chances of survival in the wild.

BACK TO THE FUTURE

WOOLLY MAMMOTHS once again roaming the Arctic. Dodoes populating islands in the Indian Ocean. Saber-toothed tigers gnashing their fangs at zoo visitors.

In 2008, researchers used the remains of several long-dead woolly mammoths to sequence the creature's genome. For the first time, they had a complete DNA picture of an extinct animal. This got the world wondering. Could a live mammoth be the next step?

Not any time soon, apparently. There are a few problems to consider. First, DNA degrades after death, so the samples used by scientists weren't perfect. If they tried to recreate a mammoth from the sequence they have now, the animal would have hundreds of thousands of mutations.

It would never develop properly. And even if scientists could create a strong, pure copy, there would be several other challenges:

- How many chromosomes does a mammoth have? The same as an elephant? Researchers have no idea.

- The mammoth DNA would have to be added to other cells—probably from frogs (which have cells that are extra-good at adapting to foreign DNA) or elephants (the best mammoth look-alikes). The cells would need to divide and grow. No one knows if that would work.

- Some sort of live animal would need to carry the pregnancy. Could an elephant mom birth a baby mammoth?

Obviously, there are lots of questions to be answered before woolly mammoths walk the earth again. But will it one day be possible? It might be too strange, too complicated, and too expensive. Then again, that's exactly what people said about walking on the moon.

IF ONLY ONE PERSON ROBBED THE JEWELRY STORE, BUT THE TWINS HAVE NEARLY IDENTICAL DNA, HOW WILL THE DETECTIVE SOLVE THE CRIME?

PIA NUTT
SUPERMODEL,
REGULAR CUSTOMER

HAZEL NUTT
SUPERMODEL,
REGULAR CUSTOMER

HINT: It will be *nearly* impossible. Turn to page 107 to find out more.

WHODUNIT?

GENETICISTS HAVE BEEN doing wild and wonderful things with their genome know-how. Here are just a few discoveries:

- Scientists have traced all of humanity back to one region of Africa.
- They've tested Egyptian mummies to figure out the family trees of ancient pharaohs.
- They've scraped skeleton teeth for DNA in the bacteria that caused the plague.

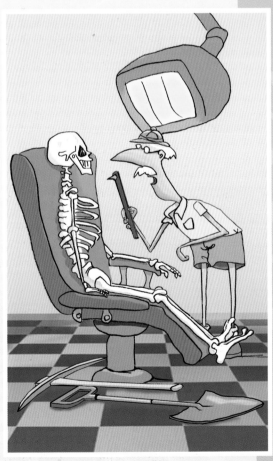

But while all of this is interesting to read about, it doesn't really affect our daily lives—or does it?

We don't necessarily think about our DNA when we visit the doctor's office, drive by the police station, or meet a long-lost cousin. But genetics are at work in all three places. And for some people, genetic research has been life-changing and even life-saving. Geneticists are helping cure disease, solve crimes, and reunite families. All of these things are probably happening right in your own town or city, right now.

BURSTING THE BUBBLE

IN 2001, young Rhys Evans was rushed to the hospital near his home in South Wales. He had pneumonia. Doctors tried an oxygen tent, but he still wasn't getting enough air. In desperation, they turned to a ventilator to force oxygen into his lungs.

Rhys had something known as "boy in the bubble" disease. Blood tests had revealed a defective gene. Because of that gene, he couldn't make his own white blood cells, so his body couldn't fend off germs. But when Rhys was transferred to a sterile room at Great Ormond Street Hospital in London, doctors there offered a tiny hope.

Thanks to their new understanding of how genes worked, scientists had found a way to inject a healthy human gene into a mouse retrovirus. A retrovirus is a miniature parasite. It invades healthy cells and tricks them into copying virus code. If the retrovirus were altered to carry a healthy human gene, then when it invaded cells, it could make those cells copy the new gene.

The treatment had worked in French trials two years before. Rhys would be the English hospital's first attempt of it. Did his parents want to try?

Desperate, they agreed. The doctors embarked on their ground-breaking procedure:

- They extracted cells from Rhys's blood marrow.
- They genetically engineered the mouse retrovirus to carry the human gamma-c gene.
- They mixed the retrovirus cells with Rhys's blood marrow cells.
- They injected the cocktail back into Rhys's system.

Then they waited. Slowly, the little boy's lungs began to clear. His body started producing white blood cells. A few months later, the toddler could play with other kids and run in the park—things he'd never done before.

Rhys became one of the first patients to be saved by genetic engineering. And as scientists increased their understanding of how genes worked—and even how to fix them—more and more people would benefit.

WARNING SIGNS

ARE YOU A MUTANT? Well, you may not have razor claws or super-speed like the X-Men mutants, but you do have mutations within you. Since every person has a unique genetic code of more than 3 billion units, a few of those units are bound to be mixed up.

Usually, these mix-ups are harmless. The healthy parts of your DNA code balance out any problems. But what if you have a family history of a genetic disease, a mutation that's been passed down through generations?

Women with a family history of breast cancer can now undergo a genetic test to tell them whether they have a mutation in their BRCA1 gene. That gene is a sort of caretaker. It's responsible for making a protein to repair damaged DNA. Without a properly working BRCA1 gene, a woman's body doesn't have the proper repair services, and tumor cells can begin to multiply. She has a 65 percent chance of developing breast cancer—often while she's still young.

Women with a family history of breast cancer often choose to have genetic testing because there are things that can be done to make cancer

Your genes have probably been tested. In hospitals, North American newborns are automatically assessed for at least two genetic disorders—one called PKU (short for phenylketonuria), which can cause brain damage, and one that causes a thyroid problem. If those disorders are caught early, they're easily treatable.

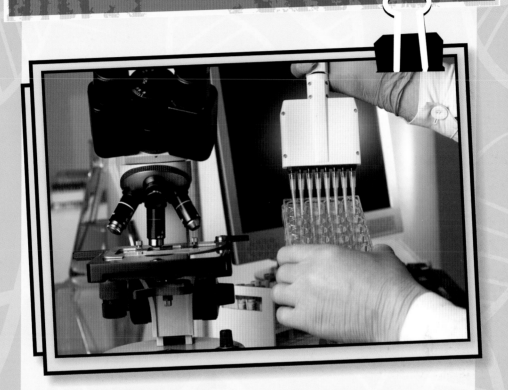

less likely. In some cases, they can have preventative radiation treatments. Other women choose surgery.

But what if you have a family history of something with less obvious treatments? For example, some people have tests to tell them whether they're at risk of early-onset dementia. A defective gene might mean they have a greater chance of losing their memory while they're still in their fifties or sixties. But there's not much they can do to change their fate, even if they know. So, is it better to know?

What would you decide?

SWITCHED ON

IN RECENT DECADES, scientists have discovered something startling about our genes. Whether or not we have a particular gene isn't always the only thing that matters. Sometimes what matters is whether or not our gene is working. That's one of the reasons identical twins can end up with slight differences.

The DNA in our cells teams up with proteins and chemical tags. Some of these proteins and chemicals are like light switches. They control genes, turning them on or off. The on/off changes don't affect the structure of DNA. Each cell still has the same instructions. But the switches *do* determine which parts of the instructions are used.

The study of our microscopic light switches is called "epigenetics." And epigenetics explains all sorts of strange things about our bodies. For instance:

- Our cells have the same DNA, but blood cells are round and fat, while nerve cells are long and thin. How do they grow differently?

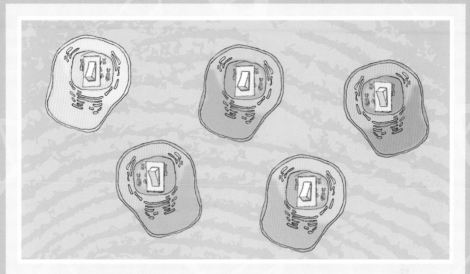

- Two identical twins live in the same home for their entire lives. But only one develops diabetes. Why?

- When mother mice are fed vitamins, the fur color of their babies changes.

  Vitamins don't change DNA, so what's happening?
  Epigenetics.

  In each of these cases, "light switches" are telling cells which genes to use and which genes to ignore.

  Scientists don't always understand why our genes are turned on or off. There's much more research to be done. But many think it has to do with our habits and our environments. Maybe the diabetic twin ate a lot of candy as a child, and that made her gene instructions work differently. Or maybe she took strong medicines, lived for a year in a different country, or worked in a stressful job. Any of these things could affect a person's on/off switches.

  As they understand epigenetics better, researchers may be able to discover chemicals that can switch genes back on, or turn them off. Even now, some labs are experimenting with medicines custom-designed for people's specific epigenetic changes.

GENERATION GAPS

HERE'S ONE OF THE STRANGEST things about epigenetics: the on/off gene changes might transfer from parent to child.

This is easy to prove in plants. If a wild radish plant is attacked by caterpillars, it grows prickly bits and gives off bad odors. Anything to chase those caterpillars away! The plant hasn't experienced a gene muta-tion. Instead, some of its on/off switches have changed.

That's when things get mysterious. The next generation of baby radishes also has prickly bits and bad smells, even if those plants are never touched by caterpillars. The parent plants have somehow passed their epigenetic changes to the baby plants.

The same sort of thing may happen in humans. For example, researchers studied harvest records from a town in northern Sweden. When young boys in the late 1800s and early 1900s had plenty of food,

their modern-day sons and grandsons had higher rates of heart disease and diabetes. When long-ago boys experienced bad harvest years and ate a little less food, their descendants were healthier.

Weird but true. The researchers suggest that when the boys overate, they changed their epigenetics. Their bodies got used to extra food. Those epigenetics were passed to sons and to grandsons, causing generations of overeating boys. Extra food led to extra weight, and eventually to higher rates of heart disease and diabetes.

It's difficult to prove these sorts of epigenetic changes in humans because we have complicated genomes and long lifespans. Obviously, it's easier to track wild radishes than human families. But many scientists are sure that epigenetics are affecting people's daily lives, and might even affect future generations.

GENETICS ROCK STAR

SUPER SLEUTH

HOW ELSE MIGHT GENES AFFECT our days? Well, that depends on whether you're planning to commit a crime this week. If you are, you might want to review the work of a British scientist named Alec Jeffreys.

In 1984, Alec was examining X-ray films of DNA. He'd been doing the same thing for years, and he'd seen patterns from baboons, lemurs, seals, cows, mice, rats, frogs, people, and plants. On this particular morning, he was looking at DNA films of a human family, searching for two things: markers called "minisatellites" that could mark a core area for comparison, and the sequence of DNA around those minisatellites.

Suddenly, Alec realized that the strands he was examining had distinct similarities and differences—and that the similarities could be used to link family members, while the differences could work as "fingerprints" to identify individuals.

He'd discovered what would soon become known as DNA fingerprinting.

After a British newspaper reported on the new technique, Alec received a call from a lawyer in London. Immigration authorities were about to deport a boy. While his family was allowed to stay in England, the boy was about to be sent back to Ghana. Apparently, his blood tests had shown that he was related *somehow* to the rest of the family but hadn't shown that he was necessarily the son. He could have been a cousin or a nephew.

Could Alec help?

With his new DNA fingerprinting technique, Alec was able to prove that mother and son were indeed members of the same immediate family. The deportation case was dropped, the boy was allowed to remain in England, and DNA fingerprinting had solved its first legal case.

In 2014, the city of Naples, Italy, announced it would be using DNA to identify dog poop left on the sidewalks. All dogs must be registered, and then a blood sample is taken, providing a DNA fingerprint. When poop is found on the sidewalk, it's sent to the lab for analysis. And if there's a DNA match between the poop and your pooch, you'll have a fine to pay!

GUILTY UNTIL PROVEN INNOCENT

IN 1970, seventeen-year-old David Milgaard was convicted of murdering a young nursing assistant, Gail Miller, in Saskatchewan. Although he insisted he was innocent, David was sentenced to life in prison. His appeal was denied. And after that, his life started to seem like a crime novel:

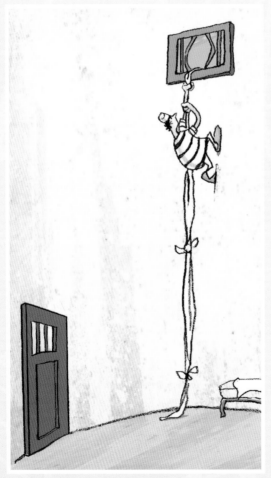

1973: He escaped from prison, only to be captured and returned.

1980: He escaped again. This time he was shot in the back, then returned.

1991: The justice minister said she wouldn't reopen his case.

1992: David was released from jail, but not declared innocent. Thanks to campaigning by his mother and intervention by the prime minister, the Supreme Court of Canada agreed to a review.

1997: DNA evidence proved David was innocent.

In the past decade, DNA has proven the innocence of more than fifteen death-row inmates in the United States—people who were about to die for their crimes. Activists worry that in cases where DNA evidence is not used, prisoners might be executed unfairly. They argue that all states should have clear laws to ensure DNA evidence is taken, used, and properly stored.

David Milgaard spent some twenty-two years behind bars. The province of Saskatchewan gave him $10 million for his trouble.

And the DNA evidence that exonerated him? It pointed to another suspect, a man who'd committed similar crimes in the past. Once again, Alec Jeffrey's DNA fingerprinting had solved a crime. Since 1984, his techniques have been used in millions of crime investigations around the world.

BODIES OF EVIDENCE

AFTER A TSUNAMI HIT Southeast Asia on December 26, 2004, more than 280,000 people died. In Phuket, Thailand, many of the dead were tourists—visitors from Asia, Europe, and North America who'd flocked to the island beaches to enjoy a winter holiday in the sun.

The tragedy left their families in far-flung corners of the world wondering what exactly had happened. They couldn't fly to Phuket—the region was in shambles. They were left scanning the TV news for clues. Were their relatives confirmed dead? Were they lost at sea, or left on the beaches? What if they were alive and injured?

Along with medical and rescue professionals, China sent a four-person team of DNA experts to help. These experts could test up to

The South Asian tsunami of 2004 strikes a beach in Thailand.

4,500 bodies a day and create a database showing the DNA of the dead. In other parts of the world, if family members chose to have their own DNA analyzed, they could then compare it to the online database. They'd discover, once and for all, if their relatives were among the tsunami's many victims.

CATALOG CONCERNS

AROUND THE WORLD, governments and police forces are keeping bigger and bigger databases of DNA. It's so useful! They can track criminals that way. Let's say someone named Sam robs a store when he's twenty years old. He's caught and convicted, and his DNA is filed. Ten years later, the police investigate a murder and find DNA evidence at the scene. When it matches Sam's DNA in the database, they know that Sam is a likely suspect.

Now imagine a slightly more complicated situation. Maybe the police find DNA at a crime scene and it doesn't match any known criminals. But they find a partial match to Sam's DNA. If the chromosomes are XX, they know that they're looking for one of Sam's female relatives; if they find XY, it's a male relative of Sam's.

In the DNA mystery within this book, a detective has rounded up suspects and asked each person to give a DNA sample. Only one person is guilty, but now all of them might have DNA stored in a database.

Is this a good thing? It might make it easier for the police to solve future crimes. But what if a government decides to use its DNA database for other things? It could give away the information to scientists, or let insurance companies peek at which people are likely to get cancer—all without permission.

In some countries, activists are working to protect people's DNA privacy. But it's such a new field, there are plenty of loopholes. So, if you were a suspect in this jewelry store robbery, should you give the police your DNA? In some countries, you'd be legally required to. In other countries, you'd have the right to choose. And in still others, a judge might decide based on the circumstances.

If you were a suspect, what would you decide?

I'VE FOUND A DNA TEST SO SENSITIVE IT CAN FIND THE TINIEST DIFFERENCES IN DNA SEQUENCING. IT CAN EVEN READ EPIGENETIC CHANGES. THIS IS THE ONLY TEST THAT CAN SPOT THE DIFFERENCE BETWEEN IDENTICAL TWINS.

YOU'RE TALKING ABOUT THAT NEWFANGLED, EXTRA-DETAILED DNA TEST. THOSE ARE EXPENSIVE.

NOT AS EXPENSIVE AS THE STOLEN JEWELS. AND WE'VE SOLVED THE CASE: THE DNA INSIDE THE GLOVE IS THAT OF PIA NUTT. SHE'LL HAVE A LOT OF EXPLAINING TO DO IN COURT.

APPARENTLY, PIA HAS BEEN OVER-SPENDING FOR YEARS AND SHE'S BROKE. BUT SHE COULDN'T STAND TO BE SEEN IN FEWER JEWELS THAN HER SISTER. SO SHE DECIDED TO STEAL SOME EXTRA. THIS CASE IS CLOSED!

CONCLUSION

THE NEXT CASE

CRIME FIGHTER OF THE YEAR! Using DNA know-how, the detective narrowed the list of jewelry store suspects. She found DNA evidence at the crime scene. She used genetic information to rule out a color-blind suspect, and cleared another based on DNA evidence stored by law enforcement. Once the lab provided all the evidence, she eliminated suspects who were male, then those of non-Scandinavian descent. And finally, she used the latest in DNA fingerprinting technology to find the thief: supermodel Pia Nutt.

DNA fingerprinting has made huge changes to how the police investigate crimes. But, as you now know, genetics research affects our lives in countless other ways. Scientists are just beginning to explore the possibilities. In coming years, they'll be researching ways to lengthen the human lifespan, address challenges in food production and world hunger, and help preserve endangered species.

While we can all agree that DNA fingerprinting is helpful, how many of its potential applications are positive? How many come with risks? And who's deciding which are which?

The first eliminated suspect is Dr. Hacker, at the end of Chapter 2.

Terry Bill disappears after Chapter 3.

At the end of chapter 4, three people are eliminated because they're male: Rusty Hammer, Stan Still, and Dwayne Pipe. Also, we lose anyone who doesn't appear Scandinavian: Dee Zaster, Daisy Picker, and Ida Gottaway.

At the end of Chapter 5, we know it's one of the twins.

At the end of Chapter 6, we identify the thief as Pia Nutt.

Have a look at these three ethical dilemmas and try to decide . . . where would you draw the line?

GENETIC DISEASE

Scientists can now discover who might be at risk of developing a disease with a genetic basis. What if . . .

- Women who are at a greater risk of breast cancer choose early treatment—whether they will ultimately develop cancer or not?

- Teens find out they're at risk of Huntington's disease, a deadly mental disorder with no cure?

- Companies and labs that perform the tests store databases with everyone's DNA results?

- Insurance companies access genetic records and refuse life insurance to people at risk of rare conditions?

TECHNO BABIES

Doctors can now discover genetic information about babies while they are still in the womb. What if . . .

- Parents choose to abort children with genetic disorders such as Down syndrome?

- Parents choose to keep boy babies and abort girls, or vice versa?

- Parents demand that researchers create genetic modifications to make their babies taller, stronger, and smarter?

DNA FINGERPRINTING

Police now collect and store DNA evidence from crimes that cause serious harm to people—crimes such as murder. What if . . .

- Police create larger databanks, storing the DNA of all major criminals?
- Even people suspected of minor crimes have their DNA cataloged?
- Countries create massive DNA databases of all citizens?
- Hackers steal the information and use other people's DNA to steal their identities, or to plant false evidence at crime scenes?

Some of these situations are already happening. Others seem a little far-fetched, but with genetic research speeding ahead, they could soon become real dilemmas. And in DNA research, some of the strangest stories have roots in truth.

TWIN TRUTHS

SO, INVESTIGATORS HAVE solved the crime! In this story, the jewelry store was robbed by one of the identical twins: Pia Nutt.

Could this sort of mystery occur in real life? Apparently, yes.

On January 25, 2009, someone stole millions of dollars' worth of jewelry from a high-end department store in Berlin. It was a heist that seemed straight out of a Hollywood movie. The thieves climbed through a second-floor window, dropped a rope ladder to the floor, then nimbly ducked the motion detectors and alarm sensors as they cracked open jewelry display cases.

They escaped the building, and no one realized the store had been robbed until early the next morning. When the police were called, they

found two clues at the scene: a rope ladder and a single glove. From the glove, they extracted a DNA sample, and the sample led them straight to . . . twins.

They arrested two twenty-seven-year-olds, Abbas and Hassan O. (In Germany, crime suspects are identified in the media only by their last initial.) The police were stumped. Abbas said it must have been Hassan who robbed the store. Hassan said it was Abbas. And the DNA samples couldn't show the difference.

A newfangled research technique could probably have given the police their answer. Researchers had recently come up with a highly sensitive (and highly expensive) way to distinguish between the DNA of twins. But the research was so new, it wasn't allowed by the rules of German courts.

No charges could be laid. It was the perfect crime.

FURTHER READING

Eamer, Claire. *Spiked Scorpions & Walking Whales*. Toronto: Annick Press, 2009.

———. *Super Crocs & Monster Wings*. Toronto: Annick Press, 2008.

Loxton, Daniel. *Evolution*. Toronto: Kids Can Press, 2010.

Marx, Christy. *Watson and Crick and DNA*. New York: Rosen Publishing Group, 2005.

Morrison, Yvonne. *The DNA Gave It Away!* New York: Scholastic, 2008.

Owen, David. *Hidden Evidence*. Buffalo, NY: Firefly Books, 2009.

Schultz, Mark. *The Stuff of Life*. New York: Hill and Wang, 2009.

Seiple, Samantha, and Todd Seiple. *Mutants, Clones, and Killer Corn*. Minneapolis, MN: Lerner Publishing Group, 2005.

Simpson, Kathleen. *Genetics: From DNA to Designer Dogs*. Washington, DC: National Geographic Children's Books, 2008.

SELECTED SOURCES

Boomsma, Dorrett, A. Busjahn, and L. Peltonen. "Classical twin studies and beyond." *Nature Reviews Genetics*, November 2002, 872–82.

Boyhan, Diane, and Henry Daniell. "Low-cost production of proinsulin in tobacco and lettuce chloroplasts for injectable or oral delivery of functional insulin and C-peptide." *Plant Biotechnology Journal*, June 2011, 585–98.

Chuan, Qin. "Beijing tests DNA from Thailand." *China Daily*, January 6, 2005, 1.

Cobb, Matthew. "Heredity before genetics: A history." *Nature Reviews Genetics*, December 2006, 953–58.

Complete Dictionary of Scientific Biography. Detroit: Charles Scribner's Sons, 2008.

Connor, Steve. "Doctors claim a first genetic 'cure' for Rhys, the boy in the bubble." *Independent*, April 4, 2002, 3.

Elkin, Lynne Osman. "Rosalind Franklin and the double helix." *Physics Today*, March 2003, 42.

Epstein, David. *The Sports Gene*. New York: Current, 2013.

Flam, Faye. "Cancer and Tasmanian devils." *Philadelphia Inquirer*, July 4, 2011, C01.

Friedberg, Errol C. "Maurice Wilkins (1916–2004)." *Molecular Cell*, December 3, 2004, 671–72.

Gill, Tony. "The atomic fish." *Humanist*, September–October 2004, 7–9.

Glynn, Jenifer. "Rosalind Franklin: 50 years on." *Notes & Records of the Royal Society*, 2008, 253–55.

Gratzer, Walter. "Obituary: Maurice Wilkins (1916–2004)." *Nature*, October 21, 2004, 922.

Haldane, John B. S. *Possible Worlds*. London: Chatto & Windus, 1927.

Hass, L. F. "Gregor Johann Mendel (1822–84)." *Journal of Neurology, Neurosurgery, and Psychiatry*, May 1998, 587.

Hawkes, Nigel. "Crick answered when immortality knocked." *London Times*, July 30, 2004, 38.

Herrera, Stephan. "Profile: Eduardo Kac." *Nature Biotechnology*, November 2005, 1331.

Hodgkinson, Kathy, E. Dicks, S. Connors, T.-L. Young, P. Parfey, and D. Pullman. "Translation of research discoveries to clinical care in arrhythmogenic right ventricular cardiomyopathy in Newfoundland and Labrador". *Genetics in Medicine*, December 2009, 859–65.

Hyde, Natalie. *DNA*. New York: Crabtree Publishing, 2010.

Iyer, V. Ramesh, and A. J. Chin. "Arrhythmogenic right ventricular cardiomyopathy/ dysplasia (ARVC/D)." *American Journal of Medical Genetics*, August 2013, 185–97.

Jegalian, Karin, and Bruce T. Lahn. "Why the Y is so weird." *Scientific American*, February 2001, 56–61.

Jeffreys, Alec J. "Genetic fingerprinting." *Nature Medicine*, October 2005, 1035–39.

Kariminejad, Mohammad H., and Ardeshir Khorshidian. "Science of breeding and heredity from ancient Persia to modern Iran." *Indian Journal of Human Genetics*, January–April 2012, 34–39.

Kieran, Mark W., Leslie Gordon, and Monica Kleinman. "New approaches to progeria." *Pediatrics*, October 1, 2007, 834–41.

Kulish, Nicholas. "Fork at end of DNA road in Berlin jewelry robbery." *International New York Times*, February 21, 2009, 2.

Luzzatto, Lucio. "Sickle cell anaemia and malaria." *Mediterranean Journal of Hematology and Infectious Diseases* 4, 1 (2012), e2012065.

McCallum, Hamish. "Tasmanian devil facial tumor disease: Lessons for conservation ecology." *Trends in Ecology and Evolution*, November 2008, 631–37.

Monsanto. "Company History." Accessed March 3, 2014. http://www.monsanto.com/ whoweare/Pages/monsanto-history.aspx.

Nathans, J., D. Thomas, and D.S. Hogess. "Molecular genetics of human color vision." *Lancet*, February 3, 1990, 263–64.

National Human Genome Research Institute. "All About the Human Genome Project." Accessed February 25, 2014. http://www.genome.gov/10001772.

Nicholls, Henry. "Darwin 200: Let's make a mammoth." *Nature*, November 2008, 310–14.

———. "Endangered species: Sex and the single rhinoceros." *Nature*, May 31, 2012, 566–69.

Offner, Susan. "The Y chromosome." *American Biology Teacher*, April 1, 2010, 235–40.

Pitman, Joanna. "Watson, Crick and the DNA double helix." *London Times*, April 19, 2008, 6.

Sindaco, R., M. Metallinou, D. Pupin, M. Fasola, and S. Carranza. "Forgotten in the ocean." *Zoologica Scripta*, July 2012, 346–62.

Stockman, James A. III. "Clinical facts and curios." *Current Problems in Pediatric and Adolescent Health Care*, August 2007, 287–93.

Toronto Star. "David Milgaard chronology." *Toronto Star*, November 30, 1991, A9.

White, Mel. "Where the weird things are." *National Geographic*, June 1, 2012, 122.

Williams, Sarah C. P. "Epigenetics." *Proceedings of the National Academy of Sciences*, February 26, 2013, 3209.

IMAGE CREDITS

INDEX

ABOUT THE AUTHOR AND ILLUSTRATOR

TANYA LLOYD KYI comes from a long genetic line of storytellers, though most of those relatives told their tales at family barbecues. Perhaps a DNA mutation prompted Tanya to put *her* stories on paper. She's now written more than 15 books for middle-grade and young-adult readers, on topics ranging from poison to underwear. Tanya lives in Vancouver, British Columbia, with her husband and their two children.

In addition to illustrating more than a dozen children's books, LIL CRUMP has created artwork for magazines, T-shirts, greeting cards, posters, and games, as well as paintings for art gallery shows. If there is an empty surface, Lil will draw or paint on it. Lil lives with her husband, daughter, and yellow dog, creating fun stuff from her studio overlooking St. Margarets Bay in Nova Scotia.